Matthew McGhee is a barrister at Twenty Essex with a broad commercial practice and a significant focus on civil fraud claims. He has been at the forefront of cyber fraud litigation, having acted for victims of cyber fraud and having both brought and defended fraud claims levelled against financial institutions. Matthew also has practical experience in cryptocurrency litigation.

Notable instructions have included *CMOC v Persons Unknown* [2018] EWHC 2230 (Comm) (a claim to trace and recover money stolen by cyber fraudsters, and the first-known occasion that a worldwide freezing injunction has been granted against 'persons unknown') and *IFT v Barclays [*2020] EWHC 3125 (Comm) (concerning a claim against the bank which received the proceeds of fraud, raising issues of when banks may be held liable for their customers' frauds).

Matthew is regularly invited to speak at national and international industry conferences and events about cyber law and litigation.

A Practical Guide to Cyber Fraud Litigation

Second Edition

A Practical Guide to Cyber Fraud Litigation

Second Edition

Matthew McGhee
of Lincoln's Inn, Barrister

Law Brief Publishing

Published 2023 by Law Brief Publishing, an imprint of Law Brief Publishing Ltd
30 The Parks
Minehead
Somerset
TA24 8BT

www.lawbriefpublishing.com

Paperback: 978-1-914608-88-9

If you forgive the fox for stealing your chickens, he will take your sheep.

— *Georgian Proverb*

PREFACE

Nearly 3 years have passed since this guide was first published and much has changed in that relatively short time:

The Covid-19 pandemic reached its zenith, providing a fertile breeding ground for cyber fraud (particularly authorised push payment fraud) as businesses operated entirely remotely and government support schemes were rolled out. The 'business' (for want of a better term) of cyber fraud has continued to become ever more professionalised, with operators of ransomware running call centres with customer service departments.

There was a proliferation in the incidence and adoption of different classes of crypto-assets, with wild swings in the value of such assets. As crypto-assets became more common, the number of cases in which they featured became more frequent and the calls for regulation or codification became louder.

There has also been increased scrutiny in banks' role in preventing – or compensating for – cyber fraud. Thus, the Contingent Reimbursement Model Code was strengthened and Confirmation of Payee was implemented. A series of cases has tested the legal obligations owed by both remitting banks and receiving banks to the victims of cyber fraud.

There remain unanswered questions in this area, with the law continuing to develop. However, it remains reassuring that the law has broadly kept pace with these rapid developments. In most cases, this has been achieved through the application of well-established principles and processes. However, new problems have in some cases demanded entirely new answers. Thus, the Law Commission is currently consulting on whether or not to create a new category of property rights for digital assets.

One issue that is frequently encountered when discussing issues around cyber fraud litigation is that many cases are, for obvious and understandable reasons (discussed in this guide), being heard in private. This means that decisions are being made, and a body of knowledge being developed, but the outcome of this is not becoming publicly available.

In many cases, these interim decisions are attended by one party only. Often, for a variety of reasons, cases do not progress from these interim phases. However, what this means is that cases which do become public may not be capable of being cited, according to the *Practice Direction (Citation of Authorities)* [2001] 1 WLR 1001. However, some decisions have for practical purposes transcended this formal bar – one example being *AA v Persons Unknown* [2020] 4 WLR 35, the first reported case where the court granted a freezing injunction in respect of cryptocurrency. This guide will refer to cases even where they may not be cited in court by reason of the Practice Direction. However, practitioners are advised to bear in mind the limited authority of such illustrations. In the case of interim applications attended by only one party, the judgment has not had the benefit of contested argument.

In preparing this second edition, I have updated the text of the previous guide – removing some sections, adding to others – to reflect the developments which I see as being of prime importance to those grappling with the issues posed by cyber fraud litigation. Significant additions include dealing with crypto-assets in their own new chapter and exploring in greater detail the ways in which a victim of cyber fraud can (or cannot) seek to hold a bank responsible for their loss.

As ever, the usual thanks are due, but are no less genuine for that. I am grateful to Law Brief Publishing for their support – before, during and following the publication of the first edition of this guide. Likewise, I repeat my previous thanks to the members of Twenty Essex for their encouragement, experience and views when writing this second edition (though, as before, any errors are mine alone). However, it is my particular privilege to thank all those who bought the first edition and demonstrated that there is the demand to justify this second edition.

I endeavour to state the law as of 30 November 2022.

Matthew McGhee
Twenty Essex, London
Cyber Monday, November 2022

CONTENTS

INTRODUCTION

What is cyber fraud?

The label 'cyber fraud' is applied to all manner of wrongdoing, but it is neither precise nor consistently applied. Similarly, there are a number of sub-species of cyber fraud, each of which have their own label (or, due to a lack of any agreed taxonomy, multiple labels), but these sub-species suffer the same failings and may also overlap. For example, this guide will consider the situation where a fraudster wrongfully accesses a commercial party's email server (a 'business email compromise fraud') in order to send replacement payment instructions to that party's legitimate counterparty. This is variously referred to as an 'invoice fraud', 'bank mandate fraud' or 'payment diversion fraud' – the multiplicity of labels, not all of which are co-extensive, is another issue encountered in this practice area.

Fraud is conventionally considered to be the use of deception in order to obtain a personal, often financial, benefit. This fits with the definition in s.1 Fraud Act 2006 which, for criminal purposes, provides that a person is guilty of fraud where they commit an offence by false representation, by failing to disclose information or by abuse of position. A classic case concerning fraud is *Cundy v Lindsay* (1878) 3 App Cas 459, which involved rogue who pretended (by an order placed on headed paper) to be a respectable business in order to acquire goods on credit from a supplier. The rogue took delivery and sold the goods on before the supplier discovered the pretence. The case concerned which of the supplier and the onward-buyer should bear the loss from the rogue's fraud.

Cyber fraud, then, might be seen as being any form of fraud which involves or pertains to computer systems or other technology. On one view, it is almost inevitable that any contemporary fraud is a 'cyber' fraud in that most modern fraudsters are likely to make use of technology at some point – for example, the modern equivalent of the rogue in *Cundy v Lindsay* would likely type rather than hand-write the letter to the supplier. However, this is not 'cyber fraud' in the way that the term is conventionally used.

Instead, cyber fraud is perhaps best understood as being a form of fraud where the use of technology is somehow integral to the fraud itself, rather than merely being an incidental means by which the fraud is perpetrated. Thus cyber fraud cases are those where the fraud is necessarily perpetrated by exploiting weaknesses in technology or would otherwise not be capable of being performed by analogue means. This distinction mirrors the approach taken by the Office of National Statistics, which separately records cyber-dependent crime (offences that can only be committed via a computer, computer network or other form of information and communications technology) and cyber-enabled crime (traditional crimes that can be increased in their scale or reach by the use of technology, but can be committed without it).

Considering the example above, the modern equivalent of *Cundy v Lindsay*, which is increasingly prevalent, is fraudsters who assume the identity of the victim to take out contracts for expensive mobile telephones, ordering (and intercepting) the delivery of the handset to the victim's address, before on-selling the handset and leaving the victim to argue with the supplier.

Moving from this cyber-enabled form of fraud to a cyber-dependent form of fraud, consider the situation where the fraudster has actually compromised the email server of the unwitting 'buyer' of the goods and causes the 'buyer' to place an order with the supplier, which the fraudster then intercepts. Here the compromise of the email server is a necessary part of the fraud.

The purpose and scope of this guide

As noted above, it is feasible that any conventional fraud may be perpetrated by cyber means. However, this does not mean that it is a 'cyber fraud'. There are other texts available which discuss fraud claims more generally and in more detail. Established principles, as set out in those other texts, may be applied to these cyber-enabled frauds. The purpose of this guide is primarily to consider those frauds which are 'cyber frauds' meeting the description in the previous section – i.e. a cyber-dependent fraud, where the use of technology is integral to the fraud itself.

That said, this guide will also consider the civil litigation angle of other related wrongdoing, even if they do not strictly amount to a fraud. There is some wrongdoing (such as extortion) which is sufficiently closely related to cyber fraud to warrant discussion in this guide. It will also be apparent that established principles fall to be applied to cyber-dependent fraud, albeit that the application is sometimes not immediately clear and will benefit from future elaboration in the courts as, inevitably, issues fall to be litigated.

The court has traditionally shown a willingness to facilitate and support fraud investigations, creating and extending its jurisprudence where required. With the advent of cyber fraud, the court has maintained that tradition. In the pursuit of justice, judges have been prepared both to apply their procedural powers in flexible and pragmatic ways and to develop established common law principles so as to respond to the novel challenges posed by cyber fraud.

This guide will consider certain specific forms of cyber fraud which have become increasingly prevalent in recent years. It will examine how current law and procedure can be deployed to combat these forms of fraud. It also ventures to predict the trend of certain areas of the law and to suggest where future litigation activity may lie.

CHAPTER ONE

COMMENCING PROCEEDINGS AGAINST ANONYMOUS FRAUDSTERS

Where a person has been the victim of a fraud, the most obvious target for any civil recovery action is the person who perpetrated that fraud in the first place.

However, one of the primary difficulties in any instance of cyber fraud is that the perpetrators may not be immediately, personally identifiable. Cyber fraudsters can remain largely anonymous, perpetrating the fraud and escaping with the proceeds before anyone is aware of the presence or identity of the fraudster. Taking the example above of a fraudster interfering with a legitimate transaction between a buyer and a seller, the buyer may unwittingly be corresponding with the fraudster (by email, for example) without being aware that the fraudster is not in fact the seller. When the buyer later discovers the fraud, the buyer may have great difficulty in discovering for itself the identity of the (now-escaped) fraudster.

This chapter considers how claims can be issued and pursued against anonymous fraudsters, explaining how those fraudsters may be identified or alternatively how recovery can be achieved even the fraudster remains stubbornly anonymous.

The options available

Broadly, there are two ways by which a prospective claimant can go about identifying and bringing proceedings against (not necessarily in that order) anonymous fraudsters:

The conventional way is for the claimant to follow a two-step process. First, the claimant will take steps to identify the anonymous fraudster. Assuming that this cannot be done by the prospective claimant's own investigations, supported as necessary by professional assistance, the prospective claimant can seek assistance from the court. In particular, the claimant can seek disclosure orders against third parties for information which might identify the fraudster. Once the fraudster has been unveiled, the claimant can issue a claim against that named fraudster in the ordinary way.

The alternative approach is for the claimant to simply issue a claim against a class of persons unknown, defined to include the anonymous fraudster, and litigate accordingly. The claimant may proceed all the way to judgment against the persons unknown, but it is also open to the claimant to take steps to identify some or all of the persons unknown in the intervening period between issuing the claim and obtaining judgment.

Each of these approaches will be discussed below. Which is more appropriate in any given case will vary on the precise facts. If speed of action is of paramount importance, such as where the fraud has recently been perpetrated, the alternative approach is often better. This is because the claim can be issued immediately and protective relief (such as freezing injunctions) obtained very quickly.

However, the alternative process does involve committing to commencing a full claim and, as will be seen, often making an array of applications. The cost of this, coupled with the inevitable risk of dissipation in cyber fraud cases, may mean that this is not a commercially feasible option for some complainants. The game may not be worth the candle. Equally, where significant sums have been misappropriated, this represents a swift and effective way to take significant steps towards making up lost ground on the fraudsters.

By contrast, the conventional approach first looks at how easy (or not) it is to identify the fraudster and any misappropriated assets. It is more targeted and thus likely to be less costly. The results of the investigation will allow a complainant to make an informed decision about whether it is worth expending further costs in pursuing the fraudster or whether the complainant is better served by considering action against persons other than those responsible for perpetrating the fraud itself. This is particularly appropriate where time is less critical, such as where a significant period of time has elapsed between the fraud itself and its discovery (or, as regrettably can happen, the complainant consulting its legal advisers as to the available options).

A further variation is where the complainant has no real interest in identifying the fraudster. If, for example, the misappropriated sums were paid into a bank account and the bank servicing that account confirms that it has already been frozen, the claimant may have no interest in uncovering the identity of the account holder. The claimant may instead prefer to simply pursue judgment against persons unknown and a proprietary order that the sums paid into the frozen account are the claimant's property and thus to be repaid.

The conventional approach to piercing anonymity

As stated above, the conventional way to bring proceedings against an anonymous fraudster is first to pierce the cloak of anonymity, before then issuing a claim against the fraudster thus-identified. The various claims which may be available against the fraudster are discussed later in this guide. This chapter focuses on the means by which the fraudster can be identified.

Disclosure pursuant to the *Norwich Pharmacal* jurisdiction

The equitable jurisdiction of the court to make disclosure orders against third parties who get mixed up in wrongdoing was established in *Norwich Pharmacal Co v Customs and Excise Commissioners* [1974] AC 133. In that case, HMRC were found to have a duty to disclose the names of patent infringers, whose goods had (innocently) passed through HMRC's hands. Lord Reid (at 175) explained the principle as follows:

> that if through no fault of his own a person gets mixed up in the tortious acts of others so as to facilitate their wrongdoing he may incur no personal liability but he comes under a duty to assist the person who has been wronged by giving him full information and disclosing the identity of the wrongdoers. I do not think that it matters whether he became so mixed up by voluntary action on his part or because it was his duty to do what he did. It may be that if this causes him expense the person seeking the information ought to reimburse him. But justice requires that he should co-operate in righting the wrong if he unwittingly facilitated its perpetration.

As summarised by Lightman J in *Mitsui & Co Ltd v Nexen Petroleum UK Ltd* [2005] 3 All ER 511 at [21]:

> The three conditions to be satisfied for the court to exercise the power to order Norwich Pharmacal relief are:
>
> i) a wrong must have been carried out, or arguably carried out, by an ultimate wrongdoer;
>
> ii) there must be the need for an order to enable action to be brought against the ultimate wrongdoer; and
>
> iii) the person against whom the order is sought must: (a) be mixed up in so as to have facilitated the wrongdoing; and (b) be able or likely to be able to provide the information necessary to enable the ultimate wrongdoer to be sued.

The first condition is relatively straightforward.

As to second condition, given that there must be a 'need' for the order before the jurisdiction is engaged, it follows that the jurisdiction should only extend to requiring the disclosure of information which is 'necessary' in order to enable action to be brought. Indeed, this is generally accepted in the analogous *Bankers Trust* jurisdiction (discussed below). This 'need'/'necessity' condition is often treated as requiring that the information sought be relevant to the intended claim. However, it arguably goes further than this and provides that the information sought shall not be required unless the intended claim could not be brought without it. Thus, highly relevant but not strictly necessary information may fall outside of the jurisdiction. This is a very strict reading of the principle, which is intended to be an exceptional remedy. However, there is a degree of flexibility in its operation and proportionality rather than strict necessity may be a better guiding rule. Suggestions that the principle is the remedy of last resort have been rejected: *Aamer v Secretary of State for Foreign & Commonwealth Affairs* [2009] EWHC 3316 (Admin) at [49]-[50] (Sullivan LJ).

As to the third condition, phrased negatively it prevents orders being obtained against 'mere witnesses' to the wrongdoing. The person from whom disclosure is sought must have done something to facilitate the wrongdoing. In the case of banks, the most common target of such orders in cyber fraud cases, the facilitation is by providing banking facilities and (ordinarily) receiving the proceeds of fraud and permitting those proceeds to be dissipated. A recent demonstration of the boundary between mere witness and innocent facilitator can be seen in *EUI Ltd v UK Vodaphone Ltd* [2021] EWCA Civ 1771.

A claim under the *Norwich Pharmacal* jurisdiction is a claim for equitable relief. The court therefore retains discretion as to whether or not to it. In *Rugby Football Union v Consolidated Information Services Ltd* [2012] 1 WLR 3333 at [17], Lord Kerr (non-exhaustively) summarised various factors which weigh in the discretion as follows (references omitted):

> The essential purpose of the remedy is to do justice. This involves the exercise of discretion by a careful and fair weighing of all relevant factors. Various factors have been identified in the authorities as relevant. These include: (i) the strength of the possible cause of action contemplated by the applicant for the order…; (ii) the strong public interest in allowing an applicant to vindicate his legal rights…; (iii) whether the making of the order will deter similar wrongdoing in the future…; (iv) whether the information could be obtained from another source…; (v) whether the respondent to the application knew or ought to have known that he was facilitating

arguable wrongdoing...; (vi) whether the order might reveal the names of innocent persons as well as wrongdoers, and if so whether such innocent persons will suffer any harm as a result...; (vii) the degree of confidentiality of the information sought...; (viii) the privacy rights under article 8 of the European Convention for the Protection of Human Rights and Fundamental Freedoms of the individuals whose identity is to be disclosed...; (ix) the rights and freedoms under the EU data protection regime of the individuals whose identity is to be disclosed...; (x) the public interest in maintaining the confidentiality of journalistic sources...

On its face, therefore, the *Norwich Pharmacal* jurisdiction is a broad one. It is often used in cases of cyber fraud to seek disclosure from banks where those banks have become mixed up in the fraud by receipt of its proceeds and are likely to have information about the subsequent whereabouts of those proceeds and the identity of the person controlling the account. However, the jurisdiction is not limited to disclosure of such information. It may also be used to seek further about the wrongdoing and its extent so as to identify the claimant's causes of action. For example, in *P v T Ltd* [1997] I WLR 1309, the court made an order for disclosure of certain information which was required for the claimant to ascertain whether it had a cause of action against a third party, and if so what.

That said, there are important limitations on the jurisdiction:

First, the claim is subject to limitations where the defendant is outside of the jurisdiction. *AB Bank v Abu Dhabi Commercial Bank* [2016] EWHC 2082 (Comm) held that none of the jurisdictional gateways then provided for in CPR PD6B para 3.1 were available, so no permission to serve the claim out of the jurisdiction could be granted. As a result, where the intended defendant is outside of the jurisdiction, there are 3 avenues by which the claimant can proceed:

(1) The claim will need to satisfy new jurisdictional gateway (25), very recently introduced. This option is discussed in a later chapter on procedural guidance.

(2) The claim will need to be served on the foreign defendant by means which do not require the court to give permission for service out of the jurisdiction. This option is discussed in a later chapter on procedural guidance.

(3) The intended relief should be sought under the independent *Bankers Trust* jurisdiction, which is discussed in the following section. Recourse may also be had to CPR 25.1(1)(g), though as discussed in the section on 'Further interim steps' below, it is unlikely that this is an instance where one of the routes above are not already available.

Second, conversely, it is not permitted to claim *Norwich Pharmacal* relief to obtain evidence for the purpose of foreign proceedings. In *Ramilos Trading v Buyanovsky* [2016] EWHC 3175 (Comm), Flaux J ruled that the existence of the Evidence (Proceedings in Other Jurisdictions) Act 1975 excludes the availability of *Norwich Pharmacal* relief in such cases. Flaux J followed the approach set out by the Court of Appeal in *R (Omar) v Secretary of State for Foreign Affairs* [2013] EWCA Civ 118, regarding the Crime (International Co-operation) Act 2003.

The reasoning in *Ramilos* refers exclusively to *Norwich Pharmacal* relief. However, the claim in that case was advanced under both the *Norwich Pharmacal* and *Bankers Trust* jurisdictions (the latter discussed in the following section). *Ramilos* is generally understood to cover both jurisdictions and the rationale for the decision applies equally to both jurisdictions.

Other jurisdictions have declined to follow the *Ramilos* approach. In the BVI case of *K&S v Z&Z* BVIHCM(COM) 2020/0016, the court held that *Norwich Pharmacal* relief was available notwithstanding that the BVI Evidence (Proceedings in Foreign Jurisdictions) 1988 as materially the same as the UK's 1975 Act. The Cayman Islands has adopted what may be an intermediate position between *Ramilos* and *K&S*. In *Arcelormittal USA LLC v Essar Global Funds Ltd* CICA (Civil) Appeal No.15 of 2019, the Cayman Islands Court of Appeal suggested that the statutory regime (there, the Evidence (Proceedings in Other Jurisdictions) (Cayman Islands) Order 1978) did not oust the *Norwich Pharamcal* jurisdiction where that latter jurisdiction was confined within its proper scope. There are good policy reasons why *Norwich Pharmacal* should remain available in these cases – e.g. to enable swift action to be taken without notice to those who are suspected of wrongdoing.

Working within the confines of *Ramilos*, Flaux J confirmed that where there is genuine uncertainty as to venue or viability of proceedings then there is no bar on seeking relief: *Shlaimoun v Mining Technologies* [2012] 1 WLR 1276. However, where the claimant is reasonably certain as to where the proceedings might take place then the *Ramilos* considerations are engaged.

As a possible exception, it might be argued that where the identity of the intended defendant (i.e. the fraudster) is unknown, it is not possible for a would-be claimant to have reached a settled view on where proceedings will be commenced. The claimant may have a firm provisional view, but if the information obtained as a result of the *Norwich Pharmacal* order points strongly towards another jurisdiction – even this jurisdiction – being the best venue, then the claimant can be expected to change their mind.

On this basis, the *Ramilos* restriction can be avoided where no proceedings have been commenced. In those circumstances, a disclosure order can be made in aid of proceedings which may take place abroad. However, the order in those circumstances should be tightly limited to that which is strictly necessary in order to identify the defendant – and so confirm whether they will be sued in this jurisdiction or elsewhere.

This argument is more difficult where proceedings have already been commenced abroad and disclosure orders are then sought in this jurisdiction to identify a new intended defendant on the basis set out above. The argument that there is an insufficiently settled intention to use the information obtained abroad is weaker because it is inherently probable that the new defendant will be joined to existing proceedings abroad, rather than be the subject of a standalone claim on the same subject matter in this jurisdiction. Indeed, the new defendant may in fact already be within a category of persons unknown already listed as a defendant in the foreign proceedings and thus, in that sense, the intended defendant may already be party to those foreign proceedings.

This draws into focus the issue with the *Ramilos* exception and the possible workaround identified here. There is a straightforward conflict between the principle identified by Flaux J (that the statutory mechanism impliedly excludes the residual common law regime) and the court's policy of enabling victims of fraud swiftly to identify – and bring proceedings against – the perpetrators.

A second, more limited possible exception to the otherwise broad rule in *Ramilos* can be seen in the English decision of *Arcelormittal USA LLC v Essar Steel Limited* [2019] 2 All ER (Comm) 414, which was distinct from the Cayman Islands proceedings mentioned above. In the English proceedings, Jacobs J held that it would not be "appropriate" to make such an order where the "*sole purpose was to facilitate enforcement proceedings abroad*". However, the court did have the power to grant relief in support of, and to make effective, an English freezing order. Thus, ancillary disclosure could be sought for this limited purpose.

Third, relief may be sought against respondents who are not considered to be wholly innocently mixed up in the wrongdoing, though the court will be careful in such cases. As a matter of principle, *Norwich Pharmacal* relief is not contingent on the respondent being innocent; that is not a barrier to relief. Thus, in *Ashworth Hospital Authority v MGN Ltd* [2002] 1 WLR 2033 at [30], Lord Woolf CJ explained that:

> what is required is involvement or participation in the wrongdoing and that if there is the necessary involvement, it does not matter that the person from whom discovery is sought was innocent and in ignorance of the wrongdoing by the person whose identity it is hoped to establish.

The judge confirmed this at [58], stating that the "*requirement*" is "*that the person from whom disclosure is sought must have been involved, whether innocently or otherwise, in the wrongdoing*".

However, care must be taken when seeking *Norwich Pharmacal* relief against persons who may be legally responsible for the wrongdoing. Although *Norwich Pharmacal* relief is not a 'last resort' route to obtain the required information, the court may consider that relief ought not to be granted against a particular respondent if that are other means by which that information could reasonably be sought. It may be that the respondent also has a privilege against self-incrimination which would operate as a partial defence to any order.

Benhurst Finance Ltd v Colliac [2018] EWHC 2188 (QB) is a recent example of *Norwich Pharmacal* relief granted against a party who was not said to be innocently involved in the wrongdoing. *Norwich Pharmacal* relief was sought against an individual who the applicant was seeking to join to separate Swiss arbitration proceedings, with the information sought by the relief being intended for use in that arbitration. The court allowed the claim for relief, ruling that there was no more suitable route to obtain the relief. It is reasonable to expect that the court will give greater scrutiny to the question of whether there is a real 'need' for *Norwich Pharmacal* relief where that relief is sought against the suspected wrongdoer, who may then be compelled to give evidence against themself.

Fourth, and linked to the previous point, when obtaining an order, the claimant will invariably be required to give undertakings to the court – including as to the use to which the disclosure will be put. It is, of course, important to ensure that the undertakings permit any use to which the claimant reasonably expects to put the information.

Where this may become contentious is where disclosure is sought from a party believed to be innocently mixed up, but who might be independently liable in the right circumstances. An example of this may be a bank which has received the proceeds of a fraud; a later chapter of this guide explores banks' potential liability in these circumstances. The bank may insist on including an undertaking that the claimant will not use any information disclosed by the bank for the purpose of proceedings against the bank. What undertakings are required in any given case is a matter within the discretion of the judge hearing the claim.

Where a claimant wants to use documents for a purpose which is barred by their undertakings, the claimant must obtain a partial release from the court to vary the undertakings that have previously been given. This is a matter between the court and the claimant, so the defendant cannot consent to a variation of the undertaking (though this will be relevant to the court's decision on whether to vary the undertakings). Claimants should be aware that 'use' of documents has been held to include both their deployment, but also the consideration of documents to decide whether those documents could be deployed: *Tchenguiz v Grant Thornton* [2017] EWHC 310 (Comm). Whether the court will permit a claimant to use documents beyond the terms of the undertakings is a discretionary matter, and the court will be principally concerned with whether there are "*special circumstances*" or a "*cogent reason*" why the use should be permitted: *Tchenguiz v Serious Fraud Office* [2014] EWCA Civ 1409. The approach of the court will be analogous to its approach to an application for permission to make collateral use of evidence pursuant to CPR 31.22.

Fifth, a potential applicant needs to give consideration as to whether or not to make the application *ex parte*. Generally, an applicant should give at least short notice to the intended respondent, even if that short notice means that the application will formally be made *ex parte* with the attendant duties of full and frank disclosure. The alternative would be to seek minimal disclosure at the *ex parte* hearing, arranging a return date to take place on full notice but relatively shortly after the initial hearing. This latter order was made in *Asiya Asset Management (Cayman) Ltd v Dipper Trading Co Ltd* [2019] HKCFI 1090, where the Hong Kong court refused to allow the full application to be made *ex parte*. The claimant was only granted disclosure which was limited to the balance of the target bank account, coupled with a non-disclosure order, pending a return date.

If an applicant does decide to make the application *ex parte*, it is necessary to demonstrate why that is required, with the court scrutinising any explanation given. In particular, the applicant will need to show either real urgency (in which case any delay in making the application should be explained) or that secrecy is justified on the basis that to make an *inter partes* application might mean that the purpose of the application will be defeated (which is likely to only be applicable where the third party against whom disclosure orders are sought is suspected, on substantial grounds, of being likely to notify the perpetrators of the underlying wrongdoing).

Disclosure pursuant to the *Bankers Trust* jurisdiction

In addition to the *Norwich Pharmacal* jurisdiction, the court has an equitable jurisdiction derived from *Bankers Trust v Shapira* [1980] 1 WLR 1274.

There is some uncertainty as to whether these two jurisdictions stem from the same or different sources. It would seem that they are separate though similar jurisdictions: *Murphy v Murphy* [1999] 1 WLR 282 at 290 (Neuberger J). In *Bankers Trust*, the later of the two decisions, *Norwich Pharmacal* was mentioned only by Lord Denning MR (at 1281), and then only in passing as an exemplar of "*the court's armoury to be able to order discovery*". By contrast, Lord Denning MR indicated (at 1282) that he considered the court to be affirming a new jurisdiction which had only been exercised in 3 unreported instances before. Notwithstanding the brevity of its mention, there are suggestions that *Bankers Trust* is founded on *Norwich Pharmacal*: *MacKinnon v Donaldson, Lufkin and Jenrette Securities Corporation* [1986] Ch 482 at 498 (Hoffmann J). The two jurisdictions have developed in parallel, applying different tests before relief can be granted, and crucially being targeted at different information. *Norwich Pharmacal* is concerned with obtaining evidence necessary to bring an action against suspected wrongdoers, whereas *Bankers Trust* is squarely concerned with identifying and tracing assets over which the claimant asserts a proprietary interest.

The apparent distinction between the jurisdictions is affirmed by the divergence between the two jurisdictions, as discussed below. In *LMN v Bitfly* [2022] EWHC 2954 (Comm) at [18], Butcher J identified the competing views but did not consider it necessary to decide whether *Bankers Trust* emanates from the *Norwich Pharmacal* principle or whether the two jurisdictions are separate lines of authority stemming from the court's underlying equitable jurisdiction (as was suggested to be the case in *AOOT Kalmneft v Denton Wilde Sapte* [2002] 1 Lloyd's Rep 417 at [11] (HHJ McGonigal)).

In *Bankers Trust*, fraudsters presented a forged cheque to Bankers Trust, who on the strength of that document paid money to the fraudsters' account with Discount Bank. Bankers Trust subsequently brought an action against Discount Bank, claiming that Discount Bank should disclose various documents relating to the fraudsters and their account. Lord Denning MR, giving the lead judgment of the Court of Appeal, held (at 1282, references omitted) that:

> So here the Discount Bank incur no personal liability: but they got mixed up, through no fault of their own, in the tortious or wrongful acts of these two men: and they come under a duty to assist the Bankers Trust Co. of New York by giving them and the court full information and disclosing the identity of the wrongdoers. In this case the particular point is "full information."
>
> This new jurisdiction must, of course, be carefully exercised. It is a strong thing to order a bank to disclose the state of its customer's account and the documents and correspondence relating to it. It should only be done when there is a good ground for thinking the money in the bank is the plaintiff's money – as for instance when the customer has got the money by fraud – or other wrongdoing – and paid it into his account at the bank. The plaintiff, who has been defrauded, has a right in equity to follow the money. He is entitled, in Lord Atkin's words, to lift the latch of the banker's door... . The customer, who has prima facie been guilty of fraud, cannot bolt the door against him.

> Owing to his fraud, he is disentitled from relying on the confidential relationship between him and the bank… . If the plaintiff's equity is to be of any avail, he must be given access to the bank's books and documents – for that is the only way of tracing the money or of knowing what has happened to it… . So the court, in order to give effect to equity, will be prepared in a proper case to make an order on the bank for their discovery. The plaintiff must of course give an undertaking in damages to the bank and must pay all and any expenses to which the bank is put in making the discovery: and the documents, once seen, must be used solely for the purpose of following and tracing the money: and not for any other purpose. With these safeguards, I think the new jurisdiction – already exercised in the three unreported cases – should be affirmed by this court.

The principles governing the *Bankers Trust* principle were summarised by Warby J in *Kyriakou v Christie Manson & Woods Ltd* [2017] EWHC 487 (QB) at [12]-[19]:

> First, there must be good grounds for concluding that the money or assets about which information is sought belonged to the claimant; secondly, there must be a real prospect that the information sought will lead to the location or preservation of such assets; and thirdly, the order should, so far as possible, be directed at uncovering the particular assets which are to be traced. … the fourth principle; namely that interests of the claimant in obtaining the order must be balanced against the possible detriment to the respondent in complying with the order, … Fifthly (and finally), it is established that the applicant must provide undertakings, first of all to pay the expenses of the Respondent in complying with the order; secondly, to compensate the respondent in damages, should loss be suffered as a result of the order; and thirdly, only to use the documents or information obtained for the purpose of tracing the assets or their proceeds.

What is notable in this statement, which is generally regarded as an authoritative summary of the relevant requirements, is that it does not require that the defendant be mixed up in the wrongdoing, a jurisdictional threshold to engage the *Norwich Pharmacal* principle. This was effectively recognised in *LMN* at [25] (Butcher J), though there are suggestions that the 'mere witness' rule does apply to *Bankers Trust* as well: e.g. *Arab Monetary Fund v Hashim (No.5)* [1992] All ER 911 at 914 (Hoffmann J). There is likewise no requirement that there be a 'need' for the order sought to enable action to be brought (though this factor would arguably form part of the analysis under Warby J's fourth principle). This tends to suggest that the *Bankers Trust* principle, at least as now understood, is distinct from *Norwich Pharmacal*.

A further observation on Warby J's second principle is that it may be met even where the party seeking disclosure knows that the assets have moved on. There does not need to be a real prospect of assets held with the disclosure target, only that the disclosure sought will enable the prospective location of such assets. Thus, in the context of a transfer of crypto-assets, it may be that the assets can be seen no longer to be associated with a particular exchange. However, disclosure against the exchange may still be sought where there is a real prospect of enabling the preservation of the assets (e.g. by identifying the account holder, who may have control over the assets in their subsequent location).

A particular strength of orders under the *Bankers Trust* jurisdiction, as compared with *Norwich Pharmacal*, is that they may be granted against parties outside of the jurisdiction notwithstanding the authority of *AB Bank* in respect of *Norwich Pharmacal* orders. In *CMOC v Persons Unknown* [2018] EWHC 2230 (Comm) (*cf.* [2017] EWHC 3599 (Comm) at [10]), such orders were made against international banks in foreign jurisdictions (i.e. not their branches within the jurisdiction) to require those banks to provide information about accounts which had received the misappropriated proceeds of a cyber fraud. Hoffmann J explained the jurisdictional basis for this in *MacKinnon v Donaldson, Lufkin and Jenrette Securities Corporation* [1986] Ch 482 at 498F-499A, confirming that the *Bankers Trust* jurisdiction has extra-territorial effect in the following terms:

> In *Bankers Trust Co. v. Shapira* the order was made against an English bank in respect of an account maintained in London. The question of international jurisdiction was not considered. However, in one of the cases cited by the Court of Appeal, *London and County Securities Ltd. (In Liquidation) v. Caplan* (unreported), 26 May 1978, Templeman J. had ordered an English bank to procure from its foreign banking subsidiaries documents relating to accounts connected with the defendant in order to trace assets which he was said to have embezzled. Templeman J. described the relief which he was granting as "onerous and ... to be granted only in the most exceptional circumstances." The exceptional circumstances were that the case was one of crime and fraud where "unless effective relief is granted, justice may well become impossible because the evidence and the fruits of crime and fraud may disappear." The foreign subsidiary banks were indemnified against liability in damages under the local law by the cross-undertaking in damages and the infringement of sovereignty was excused by a commercial equivalent of hot pursuit.
>
> In my judgment, the authorities on *Bankers Trust Co. v. Shapira* [1980] 1 W.L.R. 1274 discovery against a bank are consistent with what seems to me to be correct in principle, namely, that its international jurisdictional limits are the same as those of a subpoena duces tecum or an order under the Bankers' Books Evidence Act 1879.

The approach taken in *CMOC*, avoiding the difficulties encountered with regards *Norwich Pharmacal* orders in *AB Bank*, in respect of *Norwich Pharmacal* orders has been doubted. In *AA v Persons Unknown* [2020] 4 WLR 35 at [44]-[49], Bryan J queried whether the orders were correctly granted in *CMOC* in the face of the authority of *AB Bank*, though did not need to determine the matter on that occasion: at [69]. However, the approach in *CMOC* was followed (albeit not expressly) in *Ion Science Limited v Persons Unknown* (unreported, 21 December 2020) at [21] (Butcher J), *Fetch.ai Limited v Persons Unknown* [2021] EWHC 2254 (Comm) at [29]-[30] (HHJ Pelling

QC) and *D'Aloia v Person Unknown* [2022] EWHC 1723 (Ch) at [35]-[36] (Trower J).

At present, the position in *Mackinnon*, as applied in *CMOC* and subsequently, may be relied on. However, this distinction which has been identified has now been overtaken by an amendment to the CPR, by which a new gateway (25) has been added to CPR PD6B para 3.1. This introduces a new basis on which both *Norwich Pharmacal* and (if required) *Bankers Trust* claims can be served out of the jurisdiction in limited circumstances. It is discussed further in the procedural guidance section of this guide. However, where the gateway is not engaged, the principled approach identified in *CMOC* may still be relied on in order to serve out a claim for *Bankers Trust* relief.

Notwithstanding the new gateway (25), the distinction (if there is one) between *Norwich Pharmacal* and *Bankers Trust* remains of relevance for two reasons.

First, it is possible that disclosure orders may be sought against foreign-domiciled defendants which do not pass through the gateway but would be capable of being brought under *Bankers Trust*.

In *LMN* at [36]-[37], Butcher J expressly considered whether *Bankers Trust* orders should only be made against foreign defendants in exceptional circumstances. The judge did not decide that there was no case where exceptionality would be required, but indicated that *LMN* was not such a case because: (a) there was a possibility that the documents were within the jurisdiction; (b) the documents were electronic and thus their physical location "*of little significance*" (though this point is directly contradicted by *Gorbachev v Guriev* [2022] EWCA Civ 1270 at [83], albeit there to establish jurisdiction partly on the basis that the documents sought were in the jurisdiction); and (c) this was a case of crime and fraud (albeit not of 'hot pursuit', given that the fraud was at that time 2 years past).

Second, the closeness of the two principles affects how persuasive decisions in respect of one principle may be in respect of the other. If

Bankers Trust is a sub-species of *Norwich Pharmacal*, decisions on the type of disclosure orders which are permitted under the former should likewise provide an illustration of what is permitted under the latter. However, the view expressed above is that the jurisdictions have developed in parallel, such that it is not possible to directly cross-apply illustrations in this way.

Terms of disclosure orders

Naturally, it is advisable that a party seeking disclosure orders is as specific as reasonably practicable as to the information and documents sought by the order. The claimant should ensure that the terms of the disclosure order sought are clear and specific, targeted at information or documents to which the claimant considers it is entitled and which is reasonably necessary for the order's purpose (such as discovering the identity of the fraudster, or uncovering details of the fraud as perpetrated).

The claimant may wish to make an allowance for documents which would be disclosable (i.e. meeting the description of documents to be disclosed under the order) but for some other characteristic. A common example of such a characteristic is privilege; it is good practice to include an express exception to the disclosure obligation imposed by the order where the disclosing party considers that an otherwise-disclosable document is privileged. The order can provide that the disclosing party is permitted to withhold such documents, provided that the party notify the claimant of the general nature of the document and (in broad terms) the reason why the disclosing party considers that it is entitled to withhold disclosure of the same. The claimant can then decide whether it wishes to probe, or challenge, the reason given by the disclosing party.

A further protection which an applicant may wish to consider including as part of a disclosure order is imposing confidentiality obligations in respect of material disclosed to the applicant by the disclosing party. To take the common example of a bank giving disclosure in a case of fraud, it may be that the bank's customer (in respect of whose account the disclosure order is sought) has been innocently caught up in the wrongdoing, as the fraudster may have illicitly obtained access to the customer's account to facilitate the fraud. In such instances, the customer will have certain rights to privacy which the applicant will need to respect. To mitigate the potential injury to the rights of innocent third parties, and to facilitate the initial grant of the order (insofar as the court is required to balance the possible harm to the person whose information is to be disclosed), the applicant may wish to include provisions in the order which require the disclosed information to be kept separately and only disclosed to certain classes of person.

In circumstances where the disclosure orders are sought as the first step following discovery of the fraud, the claimant should consider whether it is appropriate to include non-disclosure orders (NDOs) as part of the disclosure order sought against the third party. The non-disclosure order may require that the third party not disclose the existence of the application or subsequent order to any party other than the third party's legal advisers. NDOs are discussed in further detail in the procedural guidance chapter of this guide. For present purposes, attention is simply drawn to the fact that the NDO may be included as much for the respondent's interests as for the claimant's. To take the common example of a bank as the third party: but for the NDO, the bank may find itself in difficulty if it freezes its client's account (by reason of the concerns raised by the claimant) and the client demands information from the bank as to why. The existence of an NDO in the disclosure order takes away the difficulty that the bank might otherwise encounter in balancing its contractual duty to provide information to its client with its obligation not to tip off the client if there is a suspicion of fraud or money laundering.

Finally, on the issue of a bank balancing competing obligations, it may be that an institution within the jurisdiction is concerned that compliance with a disclosure order may contravene 'tipping off' provisions in the Criminal Justice Act 1988, which makes it an offence to disclose to another information which was likely to prejudice a police investigation into money laundering. In *C v S* [1999] 1 WLR 1551 (CA), the court indicated that this concern was valid. Thus, an institution which has this concern should raise the matter first with the criminal investigatory authorities and then, if the authorities do not consent to disclosure, with the court so that the court can consider whether the order should be amended. To facilitate compliance with a bank's obligations, applicants for orders would be advised to include a proviso in the disclosure order, permitting the bank to withhold disclosure if they consider that they are required to do so and identifying the reason to the applicant.

When dealing with third parties in other jurisdictions, it may be advisable to consider making similar exceptions to accommodate any obligations that third party might owe under their local law. For example, again taking the example of a bank providing disclosure, there are various jurisdictions which have stringent banking secrecy laws. A claimant should avoid, so far as possible, putting the third party in a position where its obligations under an English court order and its local law obligations conflict.

The alternative approach of issuing against 'persons unknown'

The alternative approach involves issuing a Part 7 claim form which names the defendant as 'Persons Unknown'. In this way, the claim is commenced before the identity of any of the fraudsters is uncovered.

The court's general jurisdiction against persons unknown is well-established and follows from *Bloomsbury Publishing Group Limited v News Group Newspapers Ltd* [2003] 1 WLR 1633. In that case, Sir Andrew Morritt VC granted an injunction against persons unknown against a class of persons unknown, as follows (see at [4]):

> the person or persons who have offered the publishers of 'The Sun', the 'Daily Mail' and the 'Daily Mirror' newspapers a copy of the book Harry Potter and the Order of the Phoenix by J K Rowling or any part thereof and the person or persons who has or have physical possession of a copy of the said book or any part thereof without the consent of the claimants

The judge stated (at [21]) that:

> The crucial point, as it seems to me, is that the description used must be sufficiently certain as to identify both those who are included and those who are not. If that test is satisfied then it does not seem to me to matter that the description may apply to no one or to more than one person or that there is no further element of subsequent identification whether by way of service or otherwise.

In the context of cyber fraud cases, the more so as the complexity of the fraud increases, it may not be possible to include a comprehensive and succinct definition of the class of persons unknown in the abstract. It is therefore permitted to define the class of persons unknown by reference to the claim form or Particulars of Claim: *CMOC v Persons Unknown* [2018] EWHC 2230 (Comm) at [9]. However, care must be taken to ensure that the definition is no wider than necessary and that it does not capture individuals who ought not to be included: *cf. Canada Goose Retail v Persons Unknown* [2020] EWCA Civ 303 at [84]-[85]. If necessary, multiple classes of tightly defined persons unknown may need to be identified as separate defendants on the claim form.

CMOC concerned a claim against both a defined class of persons unknown (as the first defendant) and a number of identified defendants, all of whom were said to have been in some way a party to a cyber fraud. Following trial, there was a judgment against both the persons unknown and the various named defendants. This jurisdiction to bring claims against persons unknown in cases concerning "*abuse of the internet, that powerful tool for anonymous wrongdoing*", was confirmed *Cameron v Liverpool Victoria Insurance Co Ltd* [2019] 1 WLR 1471 at [11] (Lord Sumption).

However, helpful as the 'persons unknown' jurisdiction is, it should not be seen as a panacea for any difficulty in identifying the parties to a fraud. In *Cameron*, the Supreme Court explained that there are two kinds of unnameable defendants: defendants who were identifiable but whose names were unknown; and defendants who were anonymous and could not be identified. Claims can only be made against 'persons unknown' in the first category, not the second. The first category covers the defendants in *CMOC*, where it was plain that there was a perpetrator or body of conspirators operating from certain email addresses or bank accounts and the only issue was that the actual identity of such person or persons was unknown. The second category would include (in the case of *Cameron*) the unknown hit-and-run driver, but also other defendants who are not only anonymous but are also unidentifiable.

Lord Sumption, giving the lead judgment in *Cameron*, seemed to suggest that the distinction is between practical difficulties in service (which can be overcome) in the case of the first category, and insurmountable conceptual difficulties in the case of the second category: at [15]-[16]. Thus, where a person unknown is defined only by reference to acts done in the past with no way of otherwise identifying who that person was or how they can be served, whether directly or by alternate means, it may be that such a definition is not capable as sufficiently identifying the defendant for the purposes of a claim form or an application notice. This is defensible on grounds of natural justice; a claimant should not be permitted to commence a claim against a person unknown where it is conceptually impossible for that defendant to be identified and accordingly impossible for that defendant to be given the opportunity to be heard in the claim (or application) made against them.

The precise dividing line in cases of cyber fraud will be a matter for future consideration. To take the example of *Bloomsbury Publishing*, which Lord Sumption put in his first category, the definition of the persons unknown is exclusively by reference to current or former acts of the proposed defendants. This might seem contrary to Lord Sumption's statement (at [16]) that "*One does not, however, identify an unknown person simply by referring to something that he has done in the past.*" However, the judge accepted that *Bloomsbury Publishing* was a legitimate use of the person unknown jurisdiction, apparently because there was a process by which the proceedings would be brought to the attention of the persons unknown. In *Bloomsbury Publishing*, the injunction obtained enjoined the persons unknown not to take certain steps; since the injunction was granted on notice to a third party who would necessarily be involved in such steps, with the persons unknown identifying themselves when seeking to take the step, this was considered good enough.

Claimants will need to take care when bringing proceedings against persons unknown, being the perpetrators of a cyber fraud, to ensure that their claims remain on the correct side of this dividing line. This is particularly so where classes of persons unknown are defined by reference to receiving proceeds. For example, in *Jones v Persons Unknown* [2022] EWHC 2543 (Comm), one class of persons unknown was "*the individuals or companies who own or control the accounts into which the Transferred Assets were transferred other than purchasers for full value*". That definition may be defensible insofar as it is limited to the initial transfer of the misappropriated assets, but a definition which extended to the traceable proceeds would not be defensible. It would be very hard in practical terms to devise a service regime adequately notifying all recipients of traceable proceeds, and thus such a class would seem to fall into Lord Sumption's second category.

In *Canada Goose Retail v Persons Unknown* [2020] EWCA Civ 303, the Court of Appeal indicated that a third category of persons unknown may exist, in addition to Lord Sumption's categories in *Cameron*, being those anonymous persons who were highly likely to commit a future civil wrong and against whom a *quia timet* injunction was sought: at [63]. The court gave specific guidance as to how to proceed against such persons, which it characterised as including 'newcomers': at [78]-[82]. This may be of particular relevance in extortion/ransomware cases.

These principles may also be relevant where there are individuals who do not fall within Lord Sumption's first category at the time that the claim form is issued (or when an order is made against the first category persons unknown), but who by a subsequent act come within the definition of persons unknown. There is some uncertainty as to whether it is a requirement that those persons have subjective knowledge of the (for example) injunction so as to become subject to its terms, but the better view is probably that they do not: *MBR Acres Ltd v McGivern* [2022] EWHC 2072 (QB) at [64]-[70] (Nicklin J).

However, the discussion in *MBR Acres*, including Nicklin J's identification of various practical and procedural difficulties at [71]-[74], indicate the importance of both a tightly defined and closed-ended definition of persons unknown, and an effective alternative service regime to bring proceedings to the attention of all persons within the definition (not just some of the persons).

<u>Obtaining interim relief against 'persons unknown'</u>

Having issued a claim against persons unknown, the claimant is then able to apply for the same interim relief against those persons unknown as would be available to a claimant proceeding against named defendants. Such relief may be protective in nature, such as a freezing injunction, or it might instead be investigative.

Freezing injunctions

In *CMOC v Persons Unknown* [2018] EWHC 2230 (Comm) at [178]-[190], HHJ Waksman QC confirmed that the court has jurisdiction to make worldwide freezing injunctions against persons unknown. It has since been applied successfully in other cyber frauds: e.g. *World Proteins KFT v Persons Unknown* (unreported, 2 April 2019). This is a powerful development for victims of cyber fraud, where there is a particular need to take swift action to prevent the rapid dissipation of funds following their misappropriation.

The courts are willing to hear *ex parte* applications for freezing injunctions on very short notice, and may do so without the claim form having first been issued (albeit the court will almost certainly require the claim form to be issued very shortly after the freezing injunction is granted). The use of the persons unknown jurisdiction, coupled with the court's ability to hear *ex parte* applications on an emergency basis, enables a victim of cyber fraud to take steps within hours or days of discovering the fraud. Such steps will commonly include freezing the accounts into which the misappropriated sums were paid, even if the identity or involvement of the account holder remains uncertain.

In cyber fraud cases, this approach allows a claimant to take stock of their position and to make an assessment of whether it is worth pursuing the fraudsters further. A particular advantage is that the accounts can be frozen very swiftly, which maximises the chance that there are funds in the account. On ascertaining that there are frozen funds, a victim is then able to proceed with the comfort of knowing that those funds should be available to satisfy its costs incurred in pursuing the matter further. Equally, if the accounts are found to be empty, the claimant can make a decision as to whether or not to expend further time and money pursuing the fraudsters without any guarantee of recovery.

It is convenient here to mention two further aspects pertaining to freezing in connection with cyber fraud, both of which demonstrate that the courts are willing to apply their powers purposively, granting freezing injunctions to do justice to the victim of cyber fraud in circumstances where they might otherwise have refused the relief sought:

First, in cases of "*international fraud*" (not being limited to proprietary claims, but including "*serious wrongdoing comprising conduct on a large or repeated scale*") then the court "*the court would not look for such strong connecting factor with England as it would in other cases*" as a precondition to granting the relief sought: *ArcelorMittal USA LLC v Essar Steel Limited* [2019] 2 All ER (Comm) 414 (Jacobs J). In *ArcelorMittal*, there was very little connection with the jurisdiction. In such cases, the court will recognise the need to act swiftly and so may grant a freezing injunction even if only for a short interim period pending further developments – whether in the progress of the wider dispute, or so far as proceedings in other jurisdictions are concerned.

Second, the court may relax the requirement on an applicant to demonstrate that there is *prima facie* evidence of assets against which the order will operate. This requirement is a manifestation of the general rule that a court will not make an order if there is no evidence that the order will have any effect; the court will be very reluctant to make a freezing injunction if there is no evidence that the respondent has any assets to freeze.

This can be a problem in cases of cyber fraud, particularly where there is a delay in identifying and investigating the fraud and identifying the defendants. For example, it could be several weeks before the victim realises that the proceeds of the fraud were passed to a third party, but the evidence gathered at that time indicated that the recipients of payments would swiftly pass the money on to a further third partner to hinder the victim's investigation. In that case, the victim cannot say that there is *prima facie* evidence that the third party has assets, only that the third party had assets some weeks previously and is likely to have dissipated the same already. Though currently unreported, there are some instances where courts have granted freezing injunctions in these circumstances. This is justified in cases of fast-moving cyber fraud in order to do justice, not least because the most likely reason for there not being any assets would be because the intended respondent had sought to dissipate the same as part of the wider fraudulent scheme.

It is suggested that in cases of cyber fraud, particularly where the evidence shows a pattern of dissipation (or money laundering) or where the respondents have not engaged and where disclosure of the respondents' accounts is incomplete, any inability on the part of the applicant to demonstrate the availability of current assets of any respondents will not be fatal so long as the applicant has shown that the respondents did have assets and may still have those or other assets.

Similarly, where these factors are present, any delay on the part of the applicant in applying for a freezing injunction ought not to count against it. The claimant may have acted with all reasonable speed on identifying the respondent who has received the funds; thus the delay in making the application is due to the respondents' concealment of the whereabouts of the applicant's assets. However, even if the claimant has delayed following disclosure, this should not be held against it. First, delay is not a formal part of the test for a freezing injunction (unlike, for example, an anti-suit injunction). Second, it is entirely understandable that an applicant faced with a fraud should not be penalised for waiting and making a commercial decision as to when it is appropriate to make the application, balancing the perceived benefits of that application as against the cost of making it.

Proprietary injunctions

A proprietary injunction is similar to, but different in nature from, a freezing injunction. A freezing injunction prevents a respondent from using or dissipating any of their assets up to a maximum sum, usually the sum claimed by the applicant (whether as damages or otherwise). The freezing injunction is not concerned with giving the applicant security, but with preventing the respondent from making themselves judgment-proof. A proprietary injunction, by contrast, is concerned with preventing the respondent from dissipating a particular asset to which the applicant has a direct claim. A notable difference in their terms is that a respondent to a freezing injunction is ordinarily entitled to use the frozen assets for their living and legal expenses, but this presumption does not apply where a proprietary injunction is sought.

As confirmed in *Polly Peck International plc v Nadir (No 2)* [1992] 4 All ER 769, ordinary *American Cyanamid* principles apply to a proprietary injunction. First, there must be a serious issue to be tried as to whether the applicant has a proprietary interest in the property; and second, if so, the court must consider whether the balance of convenience lies in granting the relief sought. The balance of convenience involves consideration of: the efficacy of damages as an adequate remedy in the event that no order is made and the respondent dissipates the property which (it is later held) was the applicants; the adequacy of any cross-undertaking as to damages provided by the applicant; and the overall justice of the matter, including a provisional assessment of the merits of the proposed claim.

In cases of cyber fraud, it is relatively common for a claimant to make proprietary claims over certain assets – whether because the assets are said to be the claimant's property or because the assets are said to be held on trust (including constructive trust) for the claimant (including on the basis that the assets are the traceable proceeds of such assets). It is perfectly possible for a claimant to seek both a freezing injunction against a respondent, in respect of all of the respondent's assets up to the total sum claimed against that respondent, and a proprietary injunction against the same respondent, in respect of the particular property to which the applicant makes (or intends to make) a proprietary claim. In such cases, it is important to recognised that the two injunctions are likely to overlap, such that the injunction should be drafted in such a way that a respondent is clear as to what is or is not permitted.

CPR 25.1(1)(g) – disclosure, self-identification, and other orders

Where the claimant has obtained or is contemplating seeking a freezing injunction against persons unknown, it may then seek further orders under CPR 25.1(1)(g). This rule gives the court a broad power to make *"an order directing a party to provide information about the location of relevant property or assets or to provide information about relevant property or assets which are or may be the subject of an application for a freezing injunction"*. For a discussion of the scope of this power, particularly where a freezing injunction has not yet been applied for, see *Promyshlenniy Bank v Pugachev* [2016] 1 WLR 160 at [47]-[55] (Lewison LJ).

An obvious use for CPR 25.1(1)(g) would be to require a cyber fraudster to provide information about their assets (and thus the assets into which the claimant is interested in tracing their misappropriated property).

The claimant might also seek a self-identification (or 'Spartacus') order, requiring the persons unknown to identify themselves to the court. Although it may be thought unlikely that cyber fraudsters will comply with such disclosure or self-identification orders, the threat of contempt proceedings should they later be unveiled may act as a spur to prompt compliance of some individuals: *cf. PML v Persons Unknown* [2018] EWHC 838 (QB) at [17]. Further, non-compliance with the order will constitute an unlawful act which may later be relied on as part of a claim in unlawful means conspiracy: *JSC BTA Bank v Khrapunov* [2018] UKSC 19.

In addition to being an obvious adjunct to a freezing order under CPR 25.1(1)(g), it is also within the court's general jurisdiction (even absent a freezing order) to require self-identification in a proper case: *NPV v QEL* [2018] EMLR 20 at [28(ii)] (Nicklin J). Such orders are commonly attached to injunctions granted in cases of extortion (e.g. blackmail and ransomware attacks).

Search orders and similar

Search orders are powerful tools, enabling a claimant to attend without notice on a respondent's premises to secure evidence. The test for a search order was summarised in *Indicii Salus Limited v Chandreasekaran* [2006] EWHC 521 (Ch) at [85] (Warren J):

> There must be an extremely strong prima facie case; the damage potential or actual must be very serious for the applicant; there must be clear evidence that the defendants had in their possession incriminating documents or things; and there is a real possibility that the defendants may destroy such material before an on notice application is made; the harm likely to be caused by the execution of the search order on the respondent in his business affairs must not be out of proportion to the legitimate object of the order.

However, the traditional search order – particularly in cases of cyber fraud – is likely to be relegated by a new standard imaging order. In *TBD (Owen Holland) Ltd v Simons* [2021] 1 WLR 992 (CA), the Court of Appeal indicated that an imaging order will normally be the most effective means of dealing with the mischief to which a traditional search order is targeted, such that the physical search should be presumed unnecessary (and if proven otherwise, should be significantly restricted in light of the imaging order). Following the Court of Appeal's direction, a new standard form imaging order has been created.

Hyperama v Poulis [2018] EWHC 3483 (QB) is a useful reminder to parties of another investigative tool, the so-called 'doorstep delivery-up' order. This is a less-Draconian form of search order. The key difference is that the applicant is not entitled to conduct the search themselves (by their lawyers), but rather attends (without entering) the respondent's property unannounced to demand immediate delivery-up of documents or other evidence. In *Hyperama*, Pepperall J conducted a succinct review of doorstep delivery-up orders and confirmed that an "*elevated standard of whether [the court has] a high degree of assurance that [the applicant] will be able to establish its claims at trial*" applies in doorstep delivery-up orders, albeit that this is a slightly lesser standard than required for a search order (i.e. "*extremely strong prima facie case*").

In a related context, an approach analogous to search orders was taken in *Lakatamia Shipping Co Ltd v Su* [2020] 1 WLR 2852. The defendant had failed to comply with asset disclosure orders and claimed to have lost access to various email and social media accounts. The court exercised its jurisdiction under s.37(1) Senior Courts Act 1981, applying the test applicable to obtaining search order relief pre-judgment, and directed that: (1) an independent lawyer would be appointed by the court to review the contents of the accounts and to provide any non-privileged material to the claimant; and (2) the defendant must sign mandates directed to those who provided his accounts, authorising them to provide access to the lawyer so appointed.

Further interim steps

Parties should be prepared to think creatively to identify interim solutions (the example in *Lakatamia* being a good example of this). Courts have a wide variety of interim remedies available to them. One example is to permit the Land Registry to search for all properties in the name of a particular person and in respect of which the applicant has an interest. An example of this is in *Barfoot Farms Limited v Revuckas* [2021] EWHC 2423 (QB), where it was alleged that the defendants were fraudulently diverting funds from the claimant. The claimant was granted an order, permitting the Land Registry to search the list of proprietors against the names of the defendants to confirm whether there were registered assets in respect of which the claimant could seek freezing orders or seek some security.

Another example is the power to make an interim receivership order under CPR 69.2 and s.37 Senior Courts Act 1980. It is a discretionary power, to be exercised whenever it appears just and convenient to do so. The basis on which an order may be made was considered by Maurice Kay J in *JSC BTA Bank v Ablyazov* [2011] Bus LR 119 at [14]:

> It is true that the appointment of a receiver is a very intrusive remedy. It is also expensive and not easily reversible. These considerations can, however, be ameliorated by an appropriately fortified undertaking in damages. A receivership order will no doubt be completely inappropriate in the ordinary freezing order case where assets are constituted by money in bank accounts (in respect of which the relevant bank can be given notice) or by immovable property. The order will therefore only be appropriate in cases where an injunction is insufficient on its own. Such cases are only likely to arise where there is a measurable risk that, if it is not granted, a defendant will act in breach of the freezing order or otherwise seek to ensure that his assets will not be available to satisfy any judgment which may in due course be given against him.

The judge also held (at [16]-[17]) that it is not necessary for there to be "*evidence that the defendant has breached or is about to breach the terms of the freezing order made against him.*" This is a powerful tool that may be of use where a participant in the fraud (perhaps in an apparent money-laundering capacity) has identifiable assets which can be secured).

The court additionally has an inherent jurisdiction to order a party to deliver up their passport. This is an exceptional remedy and as such must be a proportionate response, such as to guard against an imminent flight risk while frozen assets are secured. The order should be no longer than necessary and must be capable referable to ensuring the effectiveness of the court's processes, which does not extend to encouraging satisfaction of a debt (judgment or otherwise).

In addition to the interim orders which may be sought against the fraudsters themselves, the claimant bringing the action against persons unknown is also able to seek disclosure orders from third parties. Such orders will commonly be to identify either the persons unknown or the whereabouts of the proceeds of the cyber fraud. The principles applicable to such orders are described above, in connection with the conventional approach, and apply equally where a claim has been issued against persons unknown.

However, where a claim has already been issued against persons unknown and a freezing injunction obtained, the claimant may additionally be able to seek disclosure pursuant to the court's jurisdiction under CPR 25.1(1)(g) (power to order a party to provide information about assets which are or may be subject to a freezing injunction). That rule may be relied on alongside the *Norwich Pharmacal* and *Bankers Trust* jurisdictions. On the face of the rule, it applies equally as a jurisdiction to make orders against third parties to the freezing injunction as it does to make orders against the respondent. This was recognised in *CMOC v Persons Unknown* [2018] EWHC 2230 (Comm) at [183] (HHJ Waksman QC).

There is, however, a limitation on the utility of CPR 25.1(1)(g): by its terms, it is concerned with "*an order directing a party to provide information*" (emphasis added). Can a person be named as a respondent under CPR 25.1(1)(g) if the only relief sought against them is under that rule? The answer is not clear but is probably 'no'. There is a separate regime in CPR 31.17 for a disclosure application against "*a person who is not a party to the proceedings*". CPR 25.1(1)(g) is thus probably not available as a route around the *AB Bank* bar on serving *Norwich Pharmacal* claims out of the jurisdiction. It was recently confirmed that CPR 31.17 applications could be served out of the jurisdiction under gateway (20): *Gorbachev v Guriev* [2022] EWCA Civ 1270. However, the judgment relied on the extra-territoriality of s.34 Senior Courts Act 1981 (concerning personal injury or death and so unlikely to be relevant in cases of cyber fraud), which provision was the basis for the CPR 31.17 application, so CPR 31.17 should not be seen as a general panacea for otherwise-unavailable disclosure against foreign parties.

Following commencement of the claim against persons unknown, the claimant may come into possession of further evidence. This evidence may follow from disclosure provided pursuant to orders made against the persons unknown or other parties, or it may arise in the course of the claimant's investigations.

Such evidence may identify named persons as being legally responsible for some part of the cyber fraud. If so, it is likely that the claimant will wish to join them as defendants to the substantive claim. Indeed, doing so would be advisable to avoid the criticisms made of the claimant in *Canada Goose Retail v Persons Unknown* [2020] 1 WLR 417 at [160]-[161] (Nicklin J).

Unless the claimant believes that it has identified all of the persons unknown, it is normally prudent to join the named defendants as additional defendants, rather than substitute the defined class of persons unknown for the known defendants. The addition of new parties can be achieved in the ordinary way under CPR 19.4.

However, it may be that the claimant has identified the entirety of the class of persons unknown (such as where the person unknown is defined as the holder of a particular bank account, with disclosure subsequently identifying that person). In that case, it is not clear whether a new defendant is being added or whether the name of an existing defendant is being amended. If the latter, the application may be made under CPR 17.1(2)(b). It would be prudent to apply under CPR 19.4 in parallel.

Given the fast pace at which cyber fraud operates and the proceeds dissipated (and thus with which a claimant's legal action will probably need to follow) it is unlikely that limitation issues will be encountered in joining new parties.

Similarly, the further evidence may identify the whereabouts of the claimant's misappropriated assets or their traceable proceeds, or it may reveal further actions taken by the fraudsters (such as the dissipation of the fraudulent proceeds by way of onward transfer to further persons unknown).

Where the claimant has identified apparent traceable proceeds of the fraud perpetrated against it, or potentially even assets which are merely identifiable assets of a named defendant, it is likely that the claimant will wish to seek further freezing injunctions over those assets. This may be coupled with further disclosure orders, such as against any third party who has or had possession of those assets, as to the current whereabouts of the assets and the identity of any further persons unknown.

It will be apparent that the claimant may be required to iterate through this process multiple times. As information is received by way of disclosure from third parties, named defendants may be joined to the proceedings and further freezing injunctions sought against those defendants. Further asset transfers to further third parties may be identified, leading to further investigations and potentially further applications for disclosure orders. In perpetrating the cyber fraud, those responsible will normally have taken steps to obscure both their identity and the final destination of the proceeds. This may be done through using shell companies, mule accounts and numerous transfers. In recent years, it has become increasingly likely that the proceeds might be converted into crypto-assets and back again, which will be addressed in a later chapter of this guide. It is therefore important to ensure that this iterative process is conducted in a targeted manner, ensuring that the steps taken (and costs incurred) are proportionate to the anticipated or hoped-for benefits.

Where a claimant iterates through this process numerous times, it may be that the court is willing to make the later orders with less scrutiny than would be applied to earlier orders where such orders are plainly justified. This is not to say that the threshold for obtaining such orders will be lowered, but it may be (for example) that certain orders which would normally require an oral hearing are granted on a paper application. This is likely only to be the case where there is a very clear case of fraud, and where the court has previously considered sufficient applications in the matter at hand, such that the court can identify a pattern and be confident that the new application is substantively a repeat of the previous applications. For example, in *Clarkson Plc v Persons Unknown* [2018] EWHC 417 (QB) at [1]-[8], Warby J explained the reasons why he was satisfied that it was appropriate to give default judgment and make a final injunction against the defendant on paper where there had been previous public hearings, no substantial change in the facts since those hearings, and no engagement by the defendant.

A final word of warning, where joining known/named defendants to proceedings against 'persons unknown': it is possible that named defendants may also come within the definition of the persons unknown. By a majority, the Court of Appeal in *Cuciureean v Secretary of State for Transport* [2022] EWCA Civ 1519 held that a person was still captured by the definition even where they were separately identified. However, Phillips LJ dissented, indicating that once a person is named on a claim form then they are outwith the class of unknown persons identified only by a definition.

CHAPTER TWO

FRAUDULENT PAYMENTS: RECOVERY FROM WRONGDOERS

Fraudulently-procured payments are the most common instance of cyber fraud, and thus perhaps the most commonly litigated – whether as against those responsible for the fraud, or as between 'innocent' parties who dispute which of them should bear the loss from the fraud.

The most obvious target for any civil recovery action in the event of a cyber fraud is the perpetrators of the fraud itself or those who assisted in the fraud. There can be difficulties in identifying and locating these wrongdoers. The previous chapter of this guide addressed how those difficulties may be overcome. This chapter considers what causes of action may be available against the wrongdoers, assuming that at least some of those responsible are named on the claim form. The next chapter addresses the options where it is, for whatever reason, not practically possible to seek recourse against wrongdoers.

In this chapter, it is sometimes necessary to distinguish between two broad categories of fraud: first, where a fraudster interferes with a relationship between two other parties (including the victim of the fraud); and second, where the only 'relationship' is between the fraudster and the victim, with no other counterparty involved.

An example of the first category concerns a legitimate relationship between a buyer and a seller of goods. The fraudster interferes with this relationship by redirecting the payment for the goods, causing the buyer to pay the fraudster rather than the seller.

An example of the second category is where a fraudster purports to be a seller of goods, causing a putative buyer to make a payment to the fraudster for non-existent goods. Another common example of this category is often referred to as 'CEO fraud', where the fraudster purports to be a senior member of the victim's organisation and directs a more junior member to make a payment at the fraudster's direction, allegedly for the organisation's business purposes.

Proprietary claim

A claimant can assert a proprietary claim over such assets as can be said in equity to be the traceable proceeds of the sums stolen from him. A proprietary claim may be very useful claim, if available, since it can both be made against anyone currently holding such assets and assist in establishing further causes of action.

The basis for the proprietary claim in cases of theft is identified in *Westdeutsche Landesbank v Islington LBC* [1996] AC 669 at 716C-D, where Lord Browne-Wilkinson stated as follows:

> I agree that the stolen moneys are traceable in equity. But the proprietary interest which equity is enforcing in such circumstances arises under a constructive, not a resulting, trust. Although it is difficult to find clear authority for the proposition, when property is obtained by fraud equity imposes a constructive trust on the fraudulent recipient: the property is recoverable and traceable in equity. Thus, an infant who has obtained property by fraud is bound in equity to restore it

Despite being the subject of much academic criticism, that *dictum* is well-established in English law and is consistent with the position adopted in other common law jurisdictions. For example, the High Court of Australia in *Black v S Freedman & Co* (1910) 12 CLR 105 (cited by Lord Goff in *Lipkin Gorman v Karpnale Ltd* [1991] 2 AC 548 at 565) held that money stolen by a husband and handed over to his wife by way of gift to her could be recovered by the victim. O'Connor J said (at 110):

> Where money has been stolen, it is trust money in the hands of the thief, and he cannot divest it of that character. If he pays it over to

> another person, then it may be followed into that other person's hands. If, of course, that other person shows that it has come to him bona fide for valuable consideration, and without notice, it then may lose its character as trust money and cannot be recovered. But if it is handed over merely as a gift, it does not matter whether there is notice or not.

Where money or other property is susceptible to a proprietary claim by reason of that property being obtained by fraud, the property is traceable in equity and the fraudster treated as a fiduciary so as to afford the victim the full range of remedies available against a defaulting trustee. The fraudster holds the property on constructive trust for the benefit of the victim.

The difficulty in the present context lies in the answer to the question; when is property "*obtained by fraud*" so as to establish a *Westdeutsche* constructive trust? This is a point which has attracted significant debate about whether and in what circumstances it is appropriate to treat a third party as a fiduciary by reason of the third party's conduct, where that third party had no prior relationship (fiduciary or otherwise) with the claimant. The niceties of this debate are outside the scope of this guide. For present purposes, it is necessary to distinguish between a number of different categories of fraudulent payment, as follows:

First, the closest analogy to Lord Browne-Wilkinson's stolen bag of coins is a cyber fraudster obtaining illicit access to the victim's bank account and directing the victim's bank to make a payment to the fraudster.

In this case, the victim does not consent to (or even know of) the transfer. In the absence of even vitiated consented to the transfer, the recipient holds the property on constructive trust for the transferor from the moment of transfer. For example, see *Armstrong DLW GmbH v Winnington Networks Ltd* [2013] Ch 156 at [127]-[129] & [273]-[277] (Stephen Morris QC) (A held B's carbon credits on constructive trust for B from the moment that A took over ministerial control of B's account).

Second, rather than the victim being unaware of (and not consenting to) the transfer, it may be that the victim's consent to the transfer the property is procured by a fraudulent misrepresentation which vitiates that consent. For example, where a cyber fraudster purports to be offering the victim a chance to participate in an initial coin offering of a cryptocurrency, but where the underlying cryptocurrency is worthless.

Where property is transferred or money paid pursuant to a contract, gift or other transaction induced by fraudulent misrepresentation, the transferor retains a right (a mere equity) to rescind the transfer. Where this right is exercised, the beneficial interest in the property is retrospectively deemed to have been re-vested in the transferor as at the time of the transfer. This allows the transferor to trace their interest in the property in the ordinary way, but may not give rise to free-standing claims for breach of fiduciary duty in respect of any intermediate transfers (though this issue is discussed further below). See *Bristol and West Building Society v Mothew* [1998] Ch 1 (CA) at 22-23 (Millett LJ).

Third, the party who procures the transfer by consent may do so by reason of non-fraudulent misrepresentation or undue influence or mistake. If so, the transfer may be subject to the same principles as the transfer in the second category described above, and thus (on rescission by the transferor) be subject to a retrospective constructive trust over the transferred property as from the date of transfer. For example, see *Bainbridge v Bainbridge* [2016] EWHC 898 (Ch).

This third category is less clearly established than the previous two. There are numerous authorities which proceed on the basis that it is correct, though the Supreme Court recently declined to confirm the position in *Re D&D Wines International Ltd* [2016] UKSC 47. What is apparent from the Supreme Court's judgment in *Re D&D Wines International Ltd* is that mere unconscionable receipt by the transferee is insufficient to found a constructive trust claim; there must be some vitiation of the transferee's position. It is inherently more likely that cases of cyber fraud will involve the first or second categories of transfer, where consent is plainly absent or vitiated, rather than this third category.

There are authorities which suggest that there is a category between the first and second categories above, where a consensual transfer is procured, but under a contract (or other instrument) which was entirely void as being "*no more than a vehicle for obtaining money … by false pretences*": *Halley v Law Society* [2003] EWCA Civ 97 at [42]-[56] (Carnwath LJ). In these circumstances, "*it is meaningless to impose a requirement for the fraudster [ie. GPG] to be notified of "rescission". From the fraudster's point of view there is nothing to rescind; for practical purposes, he has parted with nothing of value and incurred no obligations*": *Halley* at [48]. For example, where a cyber fraudster pretends to the victim that the cyber fraudster is the victim's counterparty in a contract of sale and instructs the victim to make payment under the contract to the fraudster's account.

Tracing in equity

Where a proprietary claim is established, the claimant is entitled to seek orders requiring that any traceable proceeds of the fraud be transferred to the claimant – whether those proceeds are in the hands of the fraudsters, their accomplices, or anyone else (other than a *bona fide* purchaser of the funds for value).

Equitable tracing is neither a claim nor a remedy; it is a process by which the claimant seeks to identify where, at any given time, value is located following the transfer, mixing or substitution of assets. As stated by Millett LJ in *Boscawen v Bajwa* [1996] 1 WLR 328 at 334D-E:

> It is the process by which the plaintiff traces what has happened to his property, identifies the persons who have handled or received it, and justifies his claim that the money which they handled or received (and, if necessary, which they still retain) can properly be regarded as representing his property.

The equitable tracing rules may be summarised as follows:

(a) If the bank account into which the claimant's funds were paid is made up of a mixture of the claimant's funds and the recipient's funds, drawings on that mixed fund are deemed (absent evidence of contrary intention) to be made with the recipient's own funds. It is presumed that the wrongdoer will spend his own money first before resorting to the trust fund: *Re Hallett's Estate* (1880) 13 ChD 696.

(b) The previous rule is subject to an exception where the first withdrawals from the mixed fund result in a lucrative investment which the claimant wishes to claim. In those circumstances, the claimant may elect (having regard to whatever is in his best interests – all points being taken against the recipient trustee) whether the traceable proceeds of his fund were applied to fund the investment, or whether they otherwise remained in the mixed fund: *Re Oatway* [1903] 2 Ch 356.

(c) Both of these rules are subject to this: a claimant is unable to trace beyond the lowest balance of the mixed fund after the claimant's contribution has been made: *James Roscoe (Bolton) v Winder* [1915] 1 Ch 62.

Generally, no person can pass better title in property than the title that they possess. Thus, where a person holds property subject to a trust, that person can generally only transfer the property still subject to that trust. However, the exception to this is where a person, who does not have knowledge of the tainted nature of the funds, provides goods or services in exchange for the same – i.e. a *bona fide* purchaser. They key time is when the *bona fide* purchaser provides consideration for the tainted funds; so long as this time predates the *bona fide* purchaser having knowledge, the defrauded claimant is unable to trace its property into the *bona fide* purchaser's hands.

The requirement that the *bona fide* purchaser does not have knowledge of the tainted nature of the funds is a subjective test. However, the requirement of knowledge is not limited to actual knowledge. In *Armstrong DLW GmbH v Winnington Networks Ltd* [2013] Ch 156 at [113], Stephen Morris QC explained that there were five types of knowledge:

> (1) actual knowledge; (2) wilfully shutting one's eyes to the obvious; (3) wilfully and recklessly failing to make such inquiries as an honest and reasonable man would make; (4) knowledge of circumstances which would indicate the facts to an honest and reasonable man; and (5) knowledge of circumstances which would put an honest and reasonable man on inquiry.

As to which of these types of knowledge would defeat a defence based on *bona fide* purchase for value, Stephen Morris QC confirmed (at [123]) that:

> (1) *Baden* types (1) to (3) knowledge constitute "notice" so as to defeat the defence. In order to defeat the defence on this basis, it is not necessary to show that the defendant realised that the transaction was "obviously" or "probably" improper or fraudulent; the possibility of impropriety or the claimant's interest is sufficient. (2) In other circumstances, mere negligence is not sufficient. *Baden* types (4) and (5) knowledge constitute "notice" such as to defeat this defence only if, on the facts actually known to this defendant, a reasonable person would either have appreciated that the transaction was probably fraudulent or improper, or would have made inquiries or sought advice which would have revealed the probability of impropriety.

Bona fide purchase being a defence, the burden of proof is on a defendant to demonstrate that it was a *bona fide* purchaser without notice: *Barclays Bank Plc v Boulter* [1998] 1 WLR 1 at 8-9 (Lord Hoffmann).

<u>Purpose of proprietary claim and tracing</u>

The principal purpose of asserting a proprietary claim is that it allows a claimant to seek an order requiring the defendant to hand over specifically-identified property (including the balance in a given bank account). This may be more valuable than a mere order requiring the defendant to pay damages. For example, if the claimant has frozen a specific bank account and can show the bank an order which declares that the claimant owns the money in the account, the bank may pay that balance over to the claimant without the need for the claimant to bring any enforcement proceedings or otherwise involve the defendant.

By asserting a proprietary claim and tracing the proprietary interest, a claimant will ordinarily seek a declaration of any proprietary interest established. As a general rule, the court will not make a declaration where the declaration will not serve a useful purpose: *Messier Dowty Ltd v Sabena SA* [2000] 1 WLR 2040 and *FSA v Rourke* [2002] CP Rep 14.

In *Pfizer Ltd v Roche* [2019] EWHC 1520 (Pat) at [86]-[88], Birss J recently refused to narrow the jurisdictional framework any further than this, but did indicate that the "*real purpose*" of the declaration was relevant to the exercise of discretion, explaining: "*At least as long as one is not concerned with forum shopping, the fact that the purpose is useful in relation to a dispute in a foreign court may justify granting a declaration. … There may be more than one purpose. The court will look carefully at a case in which the only or predominant purpose of the declaration sought is to use the court's judgment in foreign jurisdictions.*" A similar approach was taken in *Teva UK Ltd v Novartis AG* [2022] EWCA Civ 1617 at [51]-[52], where Arnold LJ held that "*it is wrong for an English court to make a declaration solely for the purpose of influencing a decision by a foreign court on an issue governed by the law of the foreign court*" (though "*the position might possibly be different if*" the parties did not "*have full and unimpeded access to the foreign court*").

Breach of constructive trust

Where a victim of fraud can establish a constructive trust, the constructive trustee will be subject to the same duties as any other trustee. Thus, use of trust funds for purposes other than those for the benefit of the beneficiary (i.e. the victim) will be in breach of trust and the trustee will be liable to make good any diminution in the trust assets from the trustee's own funds.

In cases of direct theft, where there was no consent on the part of the victim to the transfer, the constructive trust (as explained above) came into existence at the moment of the transfer. It is therefore probable that any dealing with the trust assets by the constructive trustee will constitute a breach of trust.

By contrast, in cases where the victim provided (vitiated) consent to the transfer and is required to rescind the transfer in order to establish a retrospective constructive trust through rescission. Although the victim can trace through any antecedent transactions prior to the rescission, it is conventionally thought that only dealings taking place after the rescission will be an independently actionable breach of the constructive trust.

There is an understandable inertia to enabling a claimant to impose, retrospectively, a trust over property and then claim damages for breach of that trust, where the actions said to constitute a breach were not wrongful prior to the claimant's rescission of the transfer. However, this inertia has been overcome for the purpose of equitable tracing, and it might be observed that the ability to impose a retrospective trust is (or should be) limited to cases where the person finding themselves to be a retrospective trustee has been involved in serious wrongdoing.

As a matter of authority, the (in)ability retrospectively to impose liability for breach of constructive trust is not clearly settled. The two cases normally cited for the proposition are *Lonrho Plc v Al-Fayed (No.2)* [1992] 1 WLR 1 (QB) and *Papamichael v National Westminster Bank* [2003] 1 Lloyd's Rep 341.

In *Lonrho (No.2)* at 11-12, Millett J held that rescinding a transfer for fraudulent misrepresentation "*cannot retrospectively subject the representor to fiduciary obligations of the kind alleged*" – namely, "*all the fiduciary obligations and disabilities of an express trustee. In particular, it was bound to abstain from placing itself in a position where its interest conflicted with its duty.*" At first blush, that seems to be a clear statement of principle which would preclude the retrospective imposition of liability.

However, when considering the factual background of *Lonrho (No.2)*, the statement of principle is not as comprehensive and preclusive as it appears to be. *Lonrho (No.2)* concerned shares. Although the legal owner of the funds might have appreciated that the seller in *Lonrho (No.2)* might elect to rescind the share sale for fraud, the seller might also be content to leave the transaction in place given that the seller had received something of value. However, that ambiguity is removed where the payor does not receive anything of value. Where, for example, a fraudster obtains payment by impersonating the payor's counterparty, the payor receives nothing of value and the payee-fraudster knows this. In these circumstances, there is no reason why a fraudster should not (and obvious policy reasons why they should) owe the full range of fiduciary duties to the payor. The situation is more akin to Lord Browne-Wilkinson's bag of stolen coins.

The second case is *Papamichael v National Westminster Bank* [2003] 1 Lloyd's Rep 341. There, Mrs Papamichael transferred money into a NatWest account by reason of the wrongdoing of Mr Papamichael. The transfer was made gratuitously, with Mrs Papamichael believing that the funds would be held for her use. They were instead held by NatWest as security for a trading account held by Mr Papamichael.

HHJ Chambers QC (at [241]-[245]) observed that a contract might operate as a "*supervening barrier*" to an immediate constructive trust, but that the same complications do not apply to a bare transfer where (as in *Papamichael*) the transferee has knowledge of the fraud. The judge's observation is taken as supporting the common reading of *Lonrho (No.2)*. However, the observation is both strictly *obiter* and a generalisation – which is unremarkable, given that the point was not in issue in *Papamichael*. As such, *Papamichael* presents no real obstacle to retrospectively characterising matters as breaches of trust.

Moreover, even if these authorities are treated as being directly on point, they only bind courts inferior to the High Court. A High Court Judge would be entitled to depart from them, though may consider the views of Millett J in particular to be highly persuasive. The point is therefore ripe for testing in an appropriate case.

Deceit

English law does not have a freestanding claim for 'fraud'. The closest equivalent is the tort of deceit. To found a claim for deceit, the claimant must show that the defendant: (a) makes a false representation; (b) which it either knows to be untrue or is reckless as whether or not it is true; (c) intends the claimant to act in reliance on the misrepresentation; and (d) causes the claimant to suffer loss in so acting: *Derry v Peek* (1889) LR 14 App Cas 337.

In some cases, the claim in deceit is clear. Consider a fraudster who causes a buyer to make a payment to the fraudster's account, rather than the buyer's counterparty, by reason of a doctored invoice. The fraudster falsely represented that the replacement bank details were the seller's, causing the claimant to pay the fraudster.

However, a significant difficulty in bringing a claim for deceit in instances of cyber fraud is that it may not be clear which particular defendant made the representation. For example, where the misrepresentations were communicated from an email address set up for the fraud, the burden is on the claimant to identify which specific defendant was operating the email account at the relevant time in order to make the specific representations relied on. It may be that the claim in deceit will only be available against a class of persons unknown.

The tort of deceit encounters a further difficulty in cases where the fraudster directly engages with the victim's bank, rather than with the victim itself. Consider the situation where a cyber fraudster has obtained illicit access to the victim's bank account and issues payment instructions, directing the victim's bank to make a payment to the fraudster. Here, the false representations are not made to the victim, but to the bank (the implicit representation here being that the fraudster is the victim, or alternatively is authorised to give instructions on behalf of the victim). The critical problem for the claimant looking to bring an action in deceit in such cases is that the fraudster intends the bank to rely on the misrepresentation. Arguably, the fraudster is uninterested in what the claimant's response to the misrepresentation would be; indeed, the fraudster might well intend that the claimant not discover that the misrepresentation has been made. However, it is (probably) the claimant, not the bank, which suffers the loss, and thus the claimant who will be seeking to reclaim the loss from the fraudster.

The solution to this further difficulty may be in the characterisation of the bank as the claimant-victim's agent for such purposes and at the relevant time (*cf. Agip Africa v Jackson* [1990] Ch 265 at 292 (Millett J)), such that representations made to the bank are to be treated as representations made to the claimant. Since the requirement that the defendant intend the claimant to act on the representation can be met where the defendant knows that, absent intervention, the claimant will so act (*Zagora Management Ltd v Zurich Insurance Plc* [2019] EWHC 140 (TCC) at [743]–[745] (HHJ Stephen Davies)), the act of the bank (in paying money out of the claimant's account) would thus be an act of the bank acting as agent for the claimant.

Dishonest assistance

A claim in dishonest assistance imposes personal liability on such persons who dishonestly either induced or assisted in the fraud – including any subsequent dealing with the funds or their traceable proceeds. In order to establish liability, a claimant must prove:

(a) The claimant is the beneficiary of a trust. This includes a constructive trust arising as a result of an impeachable transfer of the claimant's assets, as discussed above.

(b) There is a breach of trust by the trustee – again, including the constructive trustee of the fraudulently-acquired assets.

(c) The defendant to the dishonest assistance claim induced or assisted the trustee's breach of trust. The defendant must enable or induce the breach in a way that is more than of minimal importance. However, the assistance or inducement need not be necessary for the breach, nor must it necessarily result in the breach.

Each breach of trust by the trustee is capable of being induced or assisted by third parties. This is particularly relevant in cases of cyber fraud where the fraudsters will often seek to launder the proceeds of their fraud. Where A's funds are wrongfully misappropriated by B in circumstances which give rise to a constructive trust, B may transfer those funds to C with instructions that C should transfer the funds to D and so on. In this case, B is the constructive trustee of the funds for the benefit of A, and it is a breach of B's trust obligations to transfer the funds to C. C assists B's breach of trust, both in receiving the funds and in transferring those funds to D at B's instruction. The same applies to D. Thus, subject to the final requirement below, C and D can be held liable for B's breach of trust.

(d) The defendant acted dishonestly in inducing or assisting the breach of trust. This requirement is satisfied where the subjective knowledge of the defendant means that, by objective standards of honesty, the defendant knew or ought to have known that the trustee was not free to dispose of the relevant assets unencumbered. This includes both actual and 'blind eye' knowledge. It is no defence for the alleged assistant to claim either that it subjectively did not consider itself to be acting dishonestly, or that it made no enquiry whether (and thus did not confirm its suspicion that) the trustee was not free to dispose of the assets. See *Barlow Clowes International Ltd v Eurotrust International Ltd* [2005] UKPC 37, as recently applied in *Group Seven Ltd v Nasir* [2019] EWCA Civ 614 and *Payroller Ltd v Little Panda Consultants* [2020] EWHC 391 (QB).

As with any allegation of dishonesty, the constituent elements of dishonesty must be expressly pleaded: CPR PD 16 para 8.2. This includes both the matters giving rise to the defendant's subjective knowledge of the facts of the transfer and the objective reasons why the defendant's actions, given that subjective knowledge, were dishonest. In the case of corporate defendants, the Court of Appeal in *Stanford International Bank (in liquidation) v HSBC* [2021] 1 WLR 3507 (CA) (upheld on appeal) has reiterated the need to identify relevant knowledge on the part of specific natural persons, whose knowledge can then be attributed to the company.

In *Stanford*, the claimant started from the wrong end of the analysis: the claimant started from the position that transactions were made which ought not to have been made, such that the defendant bank's operations as a whole were to be characterised as dishonest. This argument was struck out at first instance, upheld on appeal.

The most obvious person whose knowledge is to be imputed to the company is its director. Indeed, where the company appears to have facilitated wrongdoing (e.g. in receiving the proceeds of a cyber fraud), it may be tempting to join the responsible director as an additional defendant. However, this requires a degree of care.

The position of directors as joint tortfeasors with their companies was discussed in *Palmer Birch v Lloyd* [2018] 4 WLR 164 at [207]-[218]. HHJ Russen QC explained that the director is not automatically liable as a joint tortfeasor, but can be if, on enquiry, "*he has been personally involved in the commissions of the tort to render him liable as a joint tortfeasor*": at [215], quoting Chadwick LJ in *MCA Records*. The judge observed that this "*will involve a detailed examination of the facts*". The litmus test is likely to be whether the director could argue that their allegedly dishonest assistance was an action in the course of the director carrying out their constitutional role within the company on a *bona fide* basis (see *Palmer Birch* at [210]). In *Barclay-Watt v Alpha Panareti Public Ltd* [2022] EWCA Civ 1169, this issue was once more considered. The Court of Appeal did not change the nature of the test, but again reiterated the fact-sensitive nature of the exercise, the need to consider existing authorities in their contexts, and the potential need to differentiate between different types of wrongdoing (with decisions in respect of one type of tort not necessarily being directly applicable to others).

Unlawful means conspiracy

A tort claim in unlawful means conspiracy imposes personal liability on such persons who participated in the relevant conspiracy – such as to perpetrate a cyber fraud on a victim. In order to establish liability, a claimant must prove:

(a) Two or more persons combined together.

(b) The combination had the intention of causing damage to a third party.

This requires that there be 'an' intention to injure a third party, but it need not be the predominant intention: *Lonrho Plc v Fayed* [1992] 1 AC 448. This requirement is met where the injury to the third party is the necessary consequence of the defendant's intention – e.g. in intending to profit from the fraud, it is a necessary consequence that the victim suffers a loss. Despite some indications otherwise, there is no need for the conspirators to identify a particular third party or to know the identity of the third party who is damaged; it is sufficient if they know that there must be a third party: *CMOC Sales and Marketing Ltd v Persons Unknown* [2018] EWHC 2230 (Comm) at [125]-[126] (HHJ Waksman QC); *ED&F Man Capital Markets Limited v Come Harvest Limited* [2022] EWHC 229 (Comm) (under appeal) (Calver J).

(c) Pursuant to the combination, a party to the combination took action which was unlawful independently of the conspiracy. The relevant 'unlawful means' can be criminal offences or any of the other civil wrongs which are claimed in the proceedings against the conspirators (such as breach of constructive trust, deceit or dishonest assistance).

(d) By reason of the unlawful act, the third party incurred loss.

There is a live issue as to whether liability for this tort requires knowledge of unlawfulness. Different lines of authority have led to conflicting High Court decisions on this point. In *Racing Partnership Ltd v Done Brothers* [2021] Ch 233 (CA), the Court of Appeal went some way towards settling this point, with the majority finding that knowledge was not a necessary element of the tort. However, Lewison LJ gave a dissenting judgment on the point and permission to appeal to the Supreme Court has been granted.

So far as the relevant unlawful means are concerned, the principal source of the relevant criminal law is the Computer Misuse Act 1990 (as amended and currently under review), which created 5 offences:

- s.1: Unauthorised access to computer material – for example, where a fraudster compromises the computer server of the victim (there is no requirement for harm to be caused);

- s.2: Unauthorised access with the intent to commit or facilitate commission of further offences – for example, where the fraudster compromises the computer server in order to send fraudulent payment instructions appearing to come directly from the victim;

- s.3: Unauthorised acts with intent to impair, or recklessness as to impairing, the operation of a computer (though not necessarily with the intent to facilitate any other criminal act) – for example, where the fraudster installs ransomware on the victim's computer system;

- s.3ZA: Unauthorised acts causing or creating risk of serious damage (though not necessarily with the intent to facilitate any other criminal act) – for example, denial of service attacks which are directed at critical public infrastructure (and thus it is less likely that this section will be relevant in civil litigation in respect of cyber fraud); and

- s.3A: Making, supplying or obtaining articles for use in offences under sections 1, 3 or 3ZA – for example, coding a computer program for a fraudster to use to compromise the victim's computer system.

s.7 Fraud Act 2006 is also of relevance to cyber frauds, as it creates an offence of making or supplying articles for use in fraud. This could be used as an extension to s.3A Computer Misuse Act 1990. Likewise, s.3 Investigatory Powers Act 2016 creates an offence of unlawfully intercepting telecommunications, which may be committed as a prelude to committing an offence under s.2 Computer Misuse Act 1990. There are also data protection offences which may be relevant – for example, s.170 Data Protection Act 2018 created an offence of deliberately or recklessly obtaining, disclosing, procuring or retaining of personal data without the consent of the data controller, or the sale (or offering for sale) of data obtained in such manner.

A final unlawful act which may be relevant in cases of cyber fraud was confirmed in *JSC BTA Bank v Khrapunov* [2018] UKSC 19. *Khrapunov* confirmed earlier judgments that a contempt of court could constitute 'unlawful means' for the purpose of this conspiracy tort. Thus, a failure to comply with a self-identification order or a disclosure order could found the tort claim, as could the breach of a freezing injunction. All of these steps can be said to be part of the conspiracy because they prolong the cover-up of the fraud, thereby obstructing the victim from identifying the whereabouts of its assets and seeking to recover against the perpetrators.

Finally, as with allegations of dishonesty, it is important to plead the full details of any conspiracy as recently reiterated by the Court of Appeal in *Elite Property Holdings v Barclays Bank* [2019] EWCA Civ 2212.

Knowing receipt

A claim in knowing receipt imposes personal liability on such persons who received the proceeds of the fraud in circumstances where it is unconscionable for such persons to retain those proceeds. In order to establish liability, a claimant must prove:

(a) Trust property is transferred in breach of trust.

(b) The property or its traceable proceeds are 'received' by the defendant. This can include receipt by an agent or nominee for the defendant, it being sufficient to found a claim in knowing receipt that the defendant has and exercises a power to direct the application of the property, even if the defendant does not in fact have direct personal control: *Manolete Partners Plc v Nag* [2022] EWHC 153 (Ch) at [92] (David Halpern QC). Notably, there is no need for the recipient to receive the property from the trustee who is acting in breach of trust, so this claim can be brought against a recipient who is several steps removed from the initial breach of trust.

(c) The defendant 'receives' the property for their own benefit.

(d) At the time of receipt (or subsequently, if the defendant is not a *bona fide* purchaser of the property), the defendant has sufficient knowledge "*to render it unconscionable for him to retain the benefit of the receipt*": *BCCI v Akindele* [2001] Ch 437 at 455 (Nourse LJ).

Unjust enrichment

A claim for restitution for unjust enrichment is likely to lie against those fraudsters who took receipt of the fraudulent payments, and potentially also or alternatively those who subsequently received the traceable proceeds of that fraud from those initial recipients.

The general requirements for liability in unjust enrichment, as summarised by Lord Reed in *Investment Trust Companies v Revenue and Customs Commissioners* [2018] AC 275 at [24] & [42], are as follows:

(a) The defendant was enriched;

(b) The defendant's enrichment was at the expense of the claimant;

(c) The enrichment was unjust; and

(d) There are no defences available to the claim.

Although the most obvious unjust enrichment claim is against any person who received the fraudulent payment directly from the victim's bank account, it is often the case that this first tier recipient has no available assets at the time that the victim freezes the fraudulent account. If so, the ability to look past any first tier recipient and to consider subsequent recipients enables the court to do justice and, critically, enhances the claimant's ability to recover the misappropriated funds from wherever the claimant happens to identify them.

That said, the claimant is required to elect between claiming against either the first tier recipient or a subsequent recipient in respect of any particular fraudulent payment. This is because if the claimant is to argue that a second tier recipient (i.e. a party who has received the proceeds of the fraud from a first tier recipient) has been unjustly enriched at the expense of the claimant, the claimant must necessarily argue that the first tier recipient was not enriched. If the first tier recipient was enriched, the subsequent enrichment of the second tier recipient was at the expense of the first tier recipient (not the claimant).

This election need not be made at the time that proceedings are commenced or Particulars of Claim pleaded. The claimant can plead a case in unjust enrichment against both the first and second tier recipients (and any third, fourth, etc. tier recipients). The claimant is then able to assess the evidence against the various recipients and identify which recipients the claimant wishes to press this claim against (which may pragmatically be determined by which recipients have assets which the claimant has been able to freeze in the proceedings). The claimant may leave the election as between the various recipients not later than the sealing of the order following judgment, so in a proper case may even seek to elect after the initial hand-down of judgment (before anything else is done), though it would be advisable to elect before this late stage. See *CMOC v Persons Unknown* [2018] EWHC 2230 (Comm) at [157]-[161] (HHJ Waksman QC); *In re L (Children) (Preliminary Finding: Power to Reverse)* [2013] UKSC 8 at [15]-[19] (Lady Hale); and *AIC Ltd v Federal Airports Authority of Nigeria* [2022] UKSC 16.

The first requirement, of enrichment, is readily established in fraudulent payment cases; the recipient of fraudulently-acquired money is thereby enriched. The second requirement, that the enrichment be at the expense of the claimant, is more difficult. This requirement was recently considered in *Investment Trust*, where Lord Reed held (at [43]) that the defendant's gain must be premised on the claimant having suffered a loss. Lord Reed continued (at [46]):

> Situations in which the defendant has received a benefit from the claimant, and the claimant has incurred a loss through the provision of that benefit, usually arise where the parties have dealt directly with one another, or with one another's property.

However, the judge added (at [47]) that there were:-

> situations in which the parties have not dealt directly with one another, or with one another's property, but in which the defendant has nevertheless received a benefit from the claimant, and the claimant has incurred a loss through the provision of that benefit. These are generally situations in which the difference from the direct provision of a benefit by the claimant to the defendant is more apparent than real.

The examples (briefly) given by Lord Reed in *Investment Trust* (at [48]) of "*non direct dealing*" included the following situations:

Shams. Lord Reed cited *Relfo Ltd (in liquidation) v Varsani* [2012] EWHC 2168 (Ch), affirmed [2014] EWCA Civ 360, as an example of a sham analysis in an unjust enrichment claim. In that case, a payment made by A to X was said to correlate to a payment made by Y to B. Although there was insufficient evidence to identify precisely what series of transactions occurred between X and Y, Sales J was satisfied that the transactions were an:

> elaborate façade to conceal what was in truth intended and arranged to be a payment for the benefit of [B]. ... The structure put in place... made it inevitable that the payment would be effected to [B]. There was no other purpose in the interim arrangements other than to conceal the true nature of the transaction.

Further to the principles set out in *Snook v London and West Riding Investments Ltd* [1967] 2 QB 786 at 802 (Diplock LJ), such transactions must be:

> intended to give to third parties or the court the appearance of creating between the parties' legal rights and obligations different from the actual legal rights and obligations (if any) which the parties intended to create.

In cases of cyber fraud, fraudulent payments are often distributed, on receipt, through a series of onward transfers to the true intended beneficiaries of the fraud. The intervening transactions will normally have no apparent purpose other than disguising the identity of the final intended recipient. This may particularly be so where the intervening recipients are shell companies or nominees who do not seem to carry on any business of their own. False documents may also be created by the fraudsters to justify onward transactions (e.g. sham invoices may be prepared solely to appease remitting and receiving banks).

Co-ordinated transactions. Lord Reed recognised (at [61]) that:

> These are cases in which, for the purpose of answering the "at the expense of" question, the court has treated a set of related transactions, operating in a co-ordinated way, as forming a single scheme or transaction, on the basis that to answer the question by considering each of the individual transactions separately would be unrealistic.

In fraudulent payment cases, there may be little (if any) difference between characterising the flow of funds as a series of sham transactions or co-ordinated transactions. The situation identified above, where payments are made through shell companies to the final recipient, may be characterised either way. Where the payments are gratuitous, it is perhaps easier to demonstrate that they are simply co-ordinated transactions such that intervening recipients can be ignored. This was the approach in *UPS Parcel Delivery Service Limited v Huaqi Import & Export Co., Limited* [2022] HKCU 4663. Where, however, the intervening transactions are notionally or claimed to be part of a wider scheme of business transactions, the court can nevertheless discount these apparent transactions as shams and treat the transfers as, in effect, having been made gratuitously.

However, where a limit on the 'co-ordinated transactions' is where the transactions are not being apparently coordinated by the suspected wrongdoers. In *Tecnimont Arabia Limited v National Westminster Bank plc* [2022] EWHC 1172 (Comm), HHJ Bird explained that the *Investment Trust* approach was intended to move from a fairness/closeness analysis to one that was more technical. In that case, the Claimant was induced by a fraud to pay money into the fraudster's account with the bank. The Claimant brought a claim in unjust enrichment against the bank. The bank successfully defended the claim on the basis that it had not been enriched by the Claimant; the transaction had taken place by the Claimant's bank debiting the Claimant's account, then there was a process of a running account operating between the two banks which meant that there was no transfer of the Claimant's funds to the receiving bank.

Agency. Where a person is interposed between the claimant and defendant, the defendant may still be liable where the interposing person received the enrichment as an actual or apparent agent for defendant. In those circumstances, the person in between the parties is "*the proxy of his principal, by virtue of the law of agency*": *Investment Trust* at [48]. Once again, where fraudulent payments cascade through various recipients who appear to be no more than nominal recipients, it may be possible in a given case to characterise the intermediary recipients as receiving agents acting for the final, intended recipient. This may be particularly so where the evidence suggests that the intermediaries are companies or trusts which are controlled by or held to the benefit of the final recipient.

Tracing. The final category of indirect receipt, identified by Lord Reed as potentially making indirect recipients amenable to claims in unjust enrichment, is:

> where the defendant receives property from a third party into which the claimant can trace an interest. Since the property is, in law, the equivalent of the claimant's property, the defendant is therefore treated as if he had received the claimant's property.

The situations where the victim of a cyber fraud can trace a proprietary interest in assets in the hands of indirect recipients are discussed in an earlier chapter of this guide.

The third requirement is that an 'unjust factor' can be identified. The relevant unjust factors in fraudulent payment cases are likely to be as follows:

Mistake. *In Barclays Bank Ltd v WJ Simms, Son and Cooke (Southern) Ltd* [1980] QB 677 at 695, Robert Goff J held that:

> If a person pays money to another under a mistake of fact which causes him to make the payment, he is prima facie entitled to recover it as money paid under a mistake of fact.

In almost every instance where a claimant brings a claim in unjust enrichment in respect of a fraudulent payment made from their account, the clamant will have made the payment operating under a mistake as to the nature of the payment – whether as to the reason why it is made or the identity of the payee or both. In the case where the cyber fraudster has caused the claimant's agent or bank to make the relevant payment without reference to the claimant themselves, the relevant mistake made by the agent or bank was made by that person as the claimant's paying agent and can accordingly be attributed to them.

For example, a bank which is instructed by a cyber fraudster to make a payment from the claimant's account only made the payment (it is assumed) by reason of the bank's mistaken belief that it had received legitimate instructions from the claimant and was authorised to make the payment.

Ignorance/No Consent. In one sense, the simplest unjust factor is the lack of consent (or even actual, rather than attributed, knowledge) of the victim. Where a cyber fraudster simply misappropriates the victim's assets, it is plain that this is an unjust factor rendering the fraudster liable in restitution. However, it may also apply to situations where a person wrongfully applies the victim's property which is under the first person's control: *Relfo Ltd (in liquidation) v Varsani* [2012] EWHC 2168 (Ch) (affirmed on appeal, though without discussion of this point: [2014] EWCA Civ 360). This applies to the case of the dishonest agent who applies the victim's funds to his own benefit rather than in accordance with the agent's mandate, but may also extend to cases where the party misapplying the property holds that property on constructive trust by reason of their earlier receipt of the assets.

Defences

The fourth requirement is that the defendant does not have a defence to the unjust enrichment claim. The possible defences in fraudulent payment cases are likely to be are as follows:

Change of position. A defendant is able to avoid liability in unjust enrichment where his "*position has so changed that it would be inequitable in all the circumstances to require him to make restitution, or alternatively restitution in full.*": *Lipkin Gorman v Karpnale Ltd* [1991] 2 AC 458 at 580 (Lord Goff).

This requires the defendant to incur a detriment in reliance on the enrichment, such as by entering into a transaction which it would not have entered into but for the enrichment. The detriment may have been incurred in advance of the actual enrichment if it was in anticipation of receiving the enrichment. However, it is normally insufficient merely to pay off a debt which was to be paid off sooner or later: *Scottish Equitable Plc v Derby* [2001] 3 All ER 818 at [35] (Robert Walker LJ). Similarly, to the extent that the detriment was the acquisition of an asset which remains in the defendant's hand at the time of the action, the defendant is still enriched and the defence may be disallowed.

A change of position defence is only open to defendants who have not acted in bad faith and who are not wrongdoers: *Lipkin Gorman* at 579 (Lord Goff). Where a defendant has a suspicion in respect of a particular transaction (as opposed to a general suspicion its counterparty might from time to time engage in suspicious transactions), good faith required the defendant to make enquiries before incurring a detriment if it wishes to be able to rely on the defence: *Abou-Rahmah v Abacha* [2007] 1 Lloyd's Rep 115 at [81] (Arden LJ). There is no need, however, for the defendant to know of or suspect the details of the specific fraud as against the claimant before the defendant is put on enquiry in this way.

As with any positive defence, including the *bona fide* purchaser defence identified below, the burden of proof is on the defendant pleading the defence.

***Bona fide* purchase.** The defence of the *bona fide* purchaser which applies in equity can also operate to exonerate a defendant otherwise liable in unjust enrichment: *Lipkin Gorman*. The principles applicable to this defence are the same as discussed above.

The distinction between the change of position defence and the separate defence of the *bona fide* purchaser lies in the extent to which each defence operates. Change of position only operates to exclude liability to the extent that there has been a change. If the defendant has only changed position in respect of half of the assets, the defence only operates to exclude liability in respect of that half. By contrast, the *bona fide* purchase defence is a complete answer to liability. If the defendant has given consideration for the enrichment, it is irrelevant that the consideration is significantly less in value than the enrichment (though if this is the case then it may be inferential evidence that the purchaser was not acting in good faith). Provided that the defendant has given some consideration in exchange for the relevant property, the claim will fail completely, whatever the disparity between the value of the property and the value of the consideration.

This defence is most frequently encountered in second (or later) layer recipients of the fraudulent proceeds. Those recipients may argue that they received the proceeds as payment for goods and services. As explained above, these alleged transactions may be shams, fabricated precisely to defeat the claimant's claim. However, even if genuine, that is not necessarily the end of the claimant's claim. Even where there is a purchase, there may be an enquiry into the recipient's *bona fides*. If there is something to put the recipient on inquiry as to the source of the funds, the defence may be defeated. Notably, in *Luk Mei Suet Michelle v Afsafari Services Company Limited* [2022] HKDC 191, HHK Kent Lee held (at [91]) that "*the risk of money laundering and cyber fraud arising from payment out of a totally unknown bank account is conspicuous and one cannot simply ignore such risk.*"

Estoppel. A claimant may be estopped from bringing a claim in unjust enrichment if it has made a relevant representation of fact to the defendant. It is difficult to see how this can be relevant in cases of cyber fraud, unless a representation has been made by the claimant since discovering the essential facts of the fraud, but it is identified here for completeness.

Recoverable losses

To the extent that a claimant has a proprietary claim to any assets, including by means of a constructive or other form of trust, they can seek an order for the delivery up of those assets. However, it is advisable also to bring claims in damages against those parties (as well as any third parties). This is for three inter-connected reasons. First, the quantum of the damages claim may exceed the value of the assets over which the claimant can assert a proprietary entitlement. Second, the claimant may find that another victim of a different fraud perpetrated by the same defendants has a competing claim to the assets over which the claimant asserts a proprietary claim. Third, the claimant is entitled to enforce a damages claim against all of a defendant's assets, not only those assets into which the claimant can trace its proprietary interest.

As described above, a claimant's non-proprietary claims are likely to be founded in tort. The damages which a claimant can claim in tort will be such as are necessary put the victim in the position as if the fraud had never happened. This requires reimbursement of all sums misappropriated, but also includes any costs or disbursements which the victim incurred as a consequence of the fraud. These disbursements can include investigation costs and the costs of legal proceedings or advice in jurisdictions other than England & Wales: *Thai Airways v KI Holdings* [2015] EWHC 1250 (Comm). Legal costs in the jurisdiction are not recoverable as damages and must instead be sought as an award of the claimant's costs in litigation in the ordinary way.

A significant benefit of the claim in tort in cases of cyber fraud is that each defendant – whether person unknown or identified defendant – may, in the right circumstances, be held jointly and severally liable for the whole sum claimed. This is so whether the defendant was the fraudster who masterminded and perpetrated the fraud directly on the victim, or whether the defendant was merely an individual who laundered some small part of the fraudulent proceeds, and includes all defendants in between. For example, where the victim is successful in its claim that there was been an unlawful means conspiracy against it, all conspirators are jointly and severally liable for the entirety of the loss caused by the conspiracy. Thus a person who is laundering money for others is part of the whole conspiracy, and liable for the whole of the losses; the conspiracy cannot usually be sub-divided into constituent parts or phases.

Interest

As to the question of interest, generally the court is only empowered to award simple interest on judgment debts. However, there is a well-established right to compound interest in respect of sums due under proprietary claims or for breaches of fiduciary duty. This also extends to claims such as knowing receipt.

There is a debate as to whether or not compound interest is available for claims for dishonest assistance. In *CMOC* at [165], HHJ Waksman QC held that it was right as a matter of principal that the penalty for dishonestly assisting a breach of trust should be the same as the penalty for the breach of trust itself, and thus be subject to compound interest. However, in *FM Capital Partners v Marino* [2019] EWHC 725 (Comm) at [27]-[35], Cockerill J considered that established authority only permitted simple interest to be recovered.

So far as claims in unjust enrichment are concerned, the Supreme Court has recently reversed the previously-established rule that the claimant was entitled to compound interest. Only simple interest can now be awarded in claims for unjust enrichment: *Prudential Assurance v HMRC* [2018] UKSC 39.

CHAPTER THREE

FRAUDULENT PAYMENTS: RECOVERY FROM 'INNOCENT' PARTIES

It may be impossible, or not commercially sensible, to pursue a fraudster in respect of a fraudulent payment. In situations where the fraudulent payment is of a category where the fraudster has redirected a legitimate payment, one of the legitimate parties to the transaction may instead take action against their counterparty or any other person who may have been innocent in respect of the fraud but whom the claimant nevertheless wishes to hold responsible for the loss.

Thus, reference here to 'innocent' parties is a reference to their being innocent of direct involvement in the fraud. Instead, the focus in this chapter is on the circumstances in which a claimant can hold these parties liable by reason of collateral wrongdoing which is indirectly connected with the fraud, or where there is some other reason (such as agency) to shift the loss on to an innocent party. However, the innocence of the possible defendant is a relevant matter, as the general policy of the law is that where there are two entirely innocent parties then the loss should lie where it falls.

In cases against 'innocent' parties, the position of the claimant may also come under scrutiny. There is scope to compare the relative fault of the two parties to determine whether (and if so, how) the loss consequent on the fraud ought to be shared. Under the Law Reform (Contributory Negligence) Act 1945, liability may be apportioned in any case where the claimant suffers damage "as the result partly of his own fault and partly of the fault" of the defendant. This partial defence is available in any claim in tort.

However, it may be that successful claims of contributory negligence will be infrequent. In *Aegis Resources DMCC v Union Bank Of India* [2020] DIFC CFI 004, the bank argued that its customer owed a duty to ensure that their email system was secure, such that that the customer was contributorily negligent when a fraudster sent false payment instructions to the bank from that email address. This argument was dismissed on the facts, the judge finding the customer to have reasonably relied on off-the-shelf software packages and to have fallen victim to a phishing attack.

Action against counterparty

This section will consider the example of a buyer and a seller of goods, where a fraudster has redirected the payment for the goods and causes the buyer to pay the fraudster rather than the seller. However, the principles discussed below are applicable to any situation where one party is obliged to pay another party, with the first party being induced by a fraud to pay the fraudster instead. The fraud can be described in a diagram, as follows:

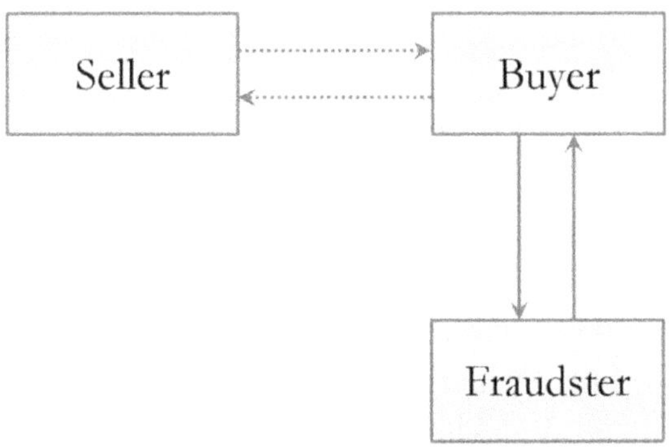

In this example, the buyer and seller were previously in direct communication (say, by email) with one another. This is shown by the dotted lines. However, the fraudster contacts the buyer (by email), who responds in kind and thereafter communication is between buyer and fraudster to the exclusion of the seller. This is shown by the solid lines. Typically, in situations such as this, the fraudster issues a replacement invoice or other payment instructions, giving the fraudster's bank details in place of the seller's. The buyer pays the fraudster, believing that it is paying the seller. This form of fraud is often termed 'invoice fraud'.

The conflict between buyer and seller arises out of the seller's continuing expectation of payment under the sale contract. Although the buyer was the party who paid the fraudster, the buyer may nonetheless feel aggrieved if it considers that the seller was in some way responsible – for example, for the means by which the fraudster either contacted the buyer or the came to know of the contract of sale between the two parties.

How the fraudster initiated contact

Confusingly similar email address

It is often the case that the initial contact between the fraudster and the buyer is by email, with the fraudster sending the buyer an email from a confusingly similar email address to that of the seller. If the seller's genuine email address was 'sales@commoditiesco.com', the fraudster might contact the buyer from the address 'sales@commodiliesco.com', the fraudster here having created a new second level domain name by replacing the 't' in 'commoditiesco' with an 'l'. Alternatively, the fraudster retains the same second level domain name ('commoditiesco'), but changes the top (or first) level domain ('com') to something else (e.g. 'co.uk').

Another, more technically sophisticated way of creating a confusingly similar email address is through the use of Punycode, creating what is known as a homograph attack. This is where non-standard characters are included in the address, but where the non-standard characters have a physical similarity with a standard character. Thus, for example, the first 'i' in 'commoditiesco' can be replaced with the non-standard character 'ı' (a dot-less i), thus: 'commodıtiesco.com'. Punycode is the standard text string which represents this domain, which in this example is 'xn--commodtiesco-64b.com'. Plainly the Punycode domain is unlikely to be confusing, but the version rendered with a non-standard character would be.

In this situation, the buyer would be able to identify the fact that an incorrect domain name was being used by the 'seller', so it is the buyer who would be at fault for failing to notice this. Put another way, there is nothing that the seller could have done to identify or prevent the fraudster using these means to contact the buyer, so it is difficult to see how it could be just to hold the seller accountable for the loss.

The only possible blame which might lie on the seller is if the fraudster discovered the existence of the transaction between seller and buyer by obtaining access to the seller's emails. However, even if so, it is difficult to see how this can found a legal basis for the buyer to rely on the confusingly similar email address. This possibility is, however, addressed in further detail later in this guide, in the section addressing action against third parties – in particular, against the source of the data used by the fraudster.

Disguised email address

Another approach which is commonly encountered is 'spoofing'. This is a technical, though relatively simple, process by which a person can send an email from email account A, but make the email look to the recipient like it is coming from email account B. It does not require the operator of email address A (i.e. the fraudster) to have access to email account B; it only requires that the operator know the address associated with email account B.

By this means, a fraudster could send an email from the email account with the address 'sales@FAKEcommoditiesco.com', but make the email appear to its recipient to have been sent by 'sales@commoditiesco.com'. The recipient would be able to see the true email address when clicking 'Reply', as this will then show the genuine email address to which the response will be sent. However, fraudsters using this means rely on recipients only checking (if at all) the email address shown on the received email.

As with confusingly similar email addresses, this has all taken place without any involvement of the person whose email address has been spoofed. The situation is essentially the same as where the recipient fails to notice a confusingly similar email address.

Genuine email address or server

Most difficult is the situation where the fraudster has actual access to the seller's email server and sends emails from that genuine server. These emails may therefore come to the buyer from the actual address which the seller had previously and genuinely used to contact the buyer. From the perspective of the buyer, this is identical to a genuine communication and the buyer has no way of discovering that the email is not coming from who it appeared to come from. The emails may also come from new email addresses which the fraudster sets up, but they key element is that they are sent from the genuine domain – e.g. the buyer may have been dealing with a person using the address 'JSmith@commoditiesco.com', with the fraudster then creating the address 'JDoe@commoditiesco.com'. By contrast with instances of confusingly similar email addresses, it is more difficult to see why the buyer is required to bear the blame given that it could not so readily identify the fraud.

The contractual obligation to pay

The starting point is that the buyer owes a debt to the seller under a contract. For so long as the debt remains unsatisfied, the creditor (seller) is entitled to call on the debtor (buyer) to make payment in accordance with the contract. The question therefore becomes whether or not the debtor's payment in line with the fraudulent instruction discharges the debt. The first question to be asked is, therefore, what is the content of the debtor's payment obligation?

The answer to this will lie in the parties' contract. It is possible that the contract, properly construed, merely requires the buyer to make payment as directed by a specified person. Alternatively, the contract may require payment to be made as directed in a message from a particular email address.

However, generally the contract will require payment in cash to the seller – i.e. granting the seller "*unconditional and unfettered right to the immediate use of the funds*": *K v A* [2019] EWHC 1118 (Comm) at [26] (Popplewell J). The obligation will normally be to pay the payee's bank with specific reference to the payee's account. In *K v A*, the contract provided that payment was to be "*to Seller's bank*", but the court had little hesitation in dismissing the argument that so long as payment was made to an account at the correct bank, it did not matter that the payment was not addressed to the account of the seller: at [27]-[31] (Popplewell J).

A further possibility may be considered: the contract might provide that payment must be made to a specific bank account. Payment other than in accordance with such an account would constitute a breach of contract, albeit that if the intended payee did in fact receive the payment then damages for breach would be nominal as the debt would be satisfied. However, it would be open to the contracting party to either vary that contract. To the extent that the fraudster seeks to vary the payment obligation, whether that binds the parties depends on whether the fraudster was acting as an agent for the receiving party at the relevant time – an issue discussed below.

It is therefore unlikely that the terms of the buyer's payment obligation will be met by the buyer making payment in accordance with a fraudulent instruction. Nevertheless, the buyer may seek to rely on the apparent nomination by the seller of replacement banking details. The question then becomes one of agency: is the fraudster, in sending the fraudulent instruction, able to bind the seller?

Actual agency – fraudster is a representative of the payee

It is possible that the fraudster has access to the seller's email server because the fraudster is an employee of the seller. In this case, the rogue employee decides to divert the employer-seller's income to the employee's own interests.

A payment to, or at the direction of, the seller's actual (or, indeed, ostensible: *Barrett v Deere* (1828) 173 ER 1131) agent can discharge the debt owed to the seller: *Sanderson v Bell* (1834) 149 ER 776. The question is thus whether an employee (or any other actual agent) of the seller binds the seller when fraudulently diverting a payment which is due to be made (and which the buyer believes is being made) to the seller's account.

Even if the agent is within the actual authority granted to them by the principal (e.g. the seller) when specifying to the principal's counterparty (i.e. the buyer) the account into which payments are to be made, it will almost certainly be outside of that authority for the agent to specify that the account is to be one held to the agent's benefit (unless the agent intends to account for that payment to the principal). This is because it is a breach of the agent's fiduciary duties to prefer the agent's interests over the principal's. Perpetrating a fraud on the principal by means of the agency granted by that principal is by definition a failure to act within the agent's obligations, and thus almost certain to be outside of the agent's authority. The agent's knowledge of the fraud negates the agent's actual authority.

However, the principal's counterparty does not have the agent's knowledge of the fraud. The question whether the principal is bound *vis-à-vis* the counterparty is a matter of the agent's ostensible agency.

Ostensible agency – fraudster is a representative of the payee

Ostensible authority was defined by Diplock LJ in *Freeman & Lockyer v Buckhurst Park Properties (Mangal) Ltd* [1964] 2 QB 480 at 503 as follows:

> An 'apparent' or ostensible authority… is a legal relationship between the principal and the contractor created by a representation, made by the principal to the contractor, intended to be and in fact acted upon by the contractor, that the agent has authority to enter on behalf of

> the principal into a contract of a kind within the scope of the 'apparent' authority, so as to render the principal liable to perform any obligations imposed upon him by such contract. To the relationship so created the agent is a stranger. He need not be (although he generally is) aware of the existence of the representation but he must not purport to make the agreement as principal himself. The representation, when acted upon by the contractor by entering into a contract with the agent, operates as an estoppel, preventing the principal from asserting that he is not bound by the contract. It is irrelevant whether the agent had actual authority to enter into the contract.

Thus, a fraudster who is an actual agent for the principal, but acts outside that actual agency in perpetrating a fraud on the principal, can nevertheless bind the principal *vis-à-vis* the principal's innocent counterparty. If a seller's finance director tells a buyer to pay the seller at an account which, unknown to the buyer, is the finance director's, the buyer is entitled to rely on the finance director's ostensible authority in claiming that the buyer's debt to the seller is discharged.

However, if the buyer is placed on notice that the apparent agent may not be acting within the scope of their agency, the buyer is not entitled to rely on this ostensible agency: *Midland Bank Ltd v Reckitt* [1933] AC 1. So if the buyer realises that the account into which payment is being made is not an account held in the seller's name, it may be that the buyer who unquestioningly makes payment into that account remains liable to pay the seller the contract price.

Ostensible agency – fraudster has obtained access to payee's servers

The more common scenario is one in which the fraudulent is a true third party who has compromised the seller's email server and obtained access that way. Save in the most unusual of cases, the fraudster in this scenario will not be an actual agent of the seller; the fraudster will be a true stranger to the seller's relationship with the buyer. However, this does not of itself preclude the fraudster from acting as the seller's agent.

The buyer could characterise the case as one of ostensible agency, with the fraudster being the seller's ostensible agent. The seller would thereby be precluded from denying the legitimacy of the instructions given by the fraudster.

There are some suggestions in the authorities that a party relying on the actions of an ostensible agent is required to take reasonable care to ensure that the ostensible agent is in fact authorised: e.g. *Galbraith & Grant Ltd v Block* [1922] 2 KB 155 at 157. This was recently questioned in a Hong Kong authority, *Akai Holdings v Kasikornbank* [2011] 1 HKC 357, which suggested that the ostensible agency may be relied on even where the party relying on it could have discovered the lack of any actual authority by the exercise of reasonable care. This authority has since been followed in England, but in *East Asia v PT Satria* [2019] UKPC 30 the Privy Council declined to follow that *Akai* so the duty to take reasonable care has probably been re-established. Although Moulder J recently applied an approach more akin to *Akai Holdings* in *Harbour Fund III, L.P. v Kazakhstan Kagazy Plc* [2021] EWHC 1128 (Comm) at [109]-[117], that appears to have been the result of a conceded position by the parties. In contrast to *Harbour Fund III*, the approach of the Privy Council was followed in *Business Mortgage Finance 6 Plc v Roundstone Technologies Ltd* [2019] EWHC 2917 (Ch) at [60]-[70] (Nugee J) and (*obiter*) in *AMP Advisory & Management Partners A.G. v Force India Formula One Team Limited* [2019] EWHC 2426 (Comm) at [83] & [103] (Moulder J).

If such a duty to take reasonable care exists, how can a buyer seek to discharge it in situations such as the present? The most obvious method, and a matter of good commercial practice in any event, would be for the buyer to verify the payment instructions following receipt (whether they be the instructions as originally provided or as varied). This would be particularly prudent if the seller's invoices or debit notes (or the covering emails for the same) carried a warning of the danger of invoice fraud or a statement that the seller either will not change its payment instructions in the course of the transaction or will not do so by email alone. Such warnings are becoming increasingly common, particularly in international business or where the consideration for payments is provided remotely.

It is unlikely that simply replying to the email providing the payment details, and seeking confirmation of the same, would be sufficient. A party purporting to act as an ostensible agent (particularly if fraudulent) will almost certainly confirm that the instructions are correct. By simply seeking confirmation, the buyer is solely relying on the security of the seller's email system. Ideally the buyer should verify the payment instructions by a different medium to the one by which they were received. So if the instructions were received by email then the buyer could telephone the seller. In some cases, this may result in the fraud being foiled, but in other cases the fraud may be sufficiently sophisticated as to intercept these verification checks. For example, if a fraudster has compromised the email server of a seller, the fraudster will also likely have access to any enquiries sent by a web form on the seller's website (which will typically be forwarded to an email account operated by the seller).

The principal difficulty with the ostensible agency argument is in demonstrating that the seller made a representation that the third party had authority to provide payment instructions. The buyer must demonstrate that the seller made some representation (even implicitly, by placing the third party in a position to present itself as an agent) to the buyer that the third party (or whoever was operating the relevant email account from time to time) was the seller's agent.

It is critical to distinguish between the person who would be expected to operate the email account (i.e. the seller's legitimate employee) and the person who operated that account to send the false payment instructions (i.e. the fraudulent third party). The employee might have actual or ostensible authority on behalf of the seller to nominate an alternative payment account. However, this is an authority of the person, not the person's email account. The email account is not a legal person and is incapable of acting as an agent. The third party is not the employee and thus cannot clothe itself in the employee's authority simply by pretending to be the employee or by operating the employee's email account.

It may be argued that the buyer has a right to presume that the seller has control of its own domain and email server, such that an email sent to an address within the seller's domain will not be accessed save with the seller's authority. This draws on the (old) authority of *Barrett v Deere* (1828) 173 ER 1131, where a person who was in the seller's counting-house and appeared to be intrusted with the seller's business there was found to have ostensible authority to receive payment to the seller. The analogy would need to be drawn between the seller in *Barrett* who had control of the physical premises and the seller in the case of cyber fraud who had control of the domain and email server.

The *Barrett* argument is probably arguable, though a related argument was dismissed in *Sell Your Car With Us Ltd v Sareen* [2019] EWHC 2332 (Ch). There, one contracting party argued that there was an implied representation by the counterparty that the counterparty would take reasonable care over the security of his email account. The contracting party argued that this implied representation was made prior to contracting when the counterparty provided his email address as the only means of contacting him. It was therefore argued that there was an actionable misrepresentation which induced the party to enter into the contract. This argument was rejected, ICC Judge Burton finding that "*When the Respondent provided his email address... he was representing no more than that he was contactable at that address.*"

If the analogy with *Barrett* can be sustained where the seller has control of its own domain and email server, can this analogy be extended to email accounts which are at domains and processed by servers which are not under the seller's control? The distinction here is between a seller, CommoditiesCo, which has its own domain (commoditiesco.com) and processes emails on its own server, and a seller which used a third-party email provider (for example, CommoditiesCo might instead do business using the email address 'commoditiesco@gmail.com'). In the case of the latter, the seller's control is limited to a username and password for the individual account, to be contrasted with a much greater degree of control in the case of the former. Given that the domain-owner in the latter case would have superior control to the seller, even over the seller's own account, it is unlikely that the latter case can be brought within the analogy of *Barrett*.

On balance, it is probably also insufficient for the buyer to rely on the mere fact that the seller exercises control over its domain and email server. The editors of Clerk & Lindsell suggest that cases such as *Barrett* are rare. Given the relative ease, or at least frequency, with which domains and email servers can be compromised, it seems unlikely that the courts will be inclined to extend the principle in *Barrett* to cover these instances. Instead, for a buyer to be able to rely on ostensible authority, it is probably necessary for the buyer to identify a further (genuine) representation made by the seller.

This analysis was followed in *J Brazil Road Contractors v Belectric Solar Ltd* (22 January 2018, unreported). The case is of limited weight and may only be cited as an authority in very limited circumstances: *Practice Direction (Citation of Authorities)* [2001] 1 WLR 1001 at [6.1]-[6.2]. However, it is instructive as to the approach of the court in a case where a BT internet email address was compromised and replacement instructions sent out. In that case, the judge ruled that there was no ostensible authority. He suggested, *obiter*, that the requirement for a representation may be met if the creditor had represented that the email address was secure (and thus, impliedly, that the debtor would not receive emails from that address which were not from an actual agent). Following this logic, it is likely that an actual or implied representation to the effect that whoever happened to be operating a particular email address (e.g. 'JSmith@commoditiesco.com', rather than J Smith themselves) had the requisite authority is required to clothe a fraudster operating that address with ostensible authority.

A further option to consider is whether a representation which post-dates, rather than pre-dates, the fraudulent communication can be said to affect the position. Consider the situation where the fraudster compromises the seller's email server and sends an email to the buyer with replacement payment instructions. What if the fraudulent email was discovered by the seller prior to the buyer making payment, but the seller failed to notify the buyer of the fraud? Such an argument was proposed in *Rijksmuseum Twenthe v Simon C Dickinson Ltd* (unreported, 30 January 2020), though was insufficiently particularised to be permitted. It would seem that there is no reason in principle why there could not be an implied representation that earlier emails were genuine, essentially an adoption by one party of emails sent by the fraudster purportedly on behalf of that party. However, to be effective the implied representation would need to be sufficiently clear to convey that adoption. It is inherently unlikely that there could be an implied representation by silence or omission.

<u>Imposition of third-party intermediaries</u>

The example of a fraudster diverting the sale proceeds under a contract becomes more complicated when, instead of the buyer, the fraudster dupes a third party who acts as some form of intermediary between the buyer and seller. Various industries commonly make use of intermediaries, with contractual counterparties communicating with one another exclusively through such intermediaries.

One or more intermediaries may be involved in any one transaction, and their roles and capacities may vary from case to case. This section will look at the possible permutations and consider what effect each has on the rights of the buyer and seller in cases of fraud.

Party agents

The most natural evolution on the direct relationship between the seller and the buyer is where each is represented by their sole agent. There are thus two agents – the buyer's and the seller's – and the analysis of who will bear the loss of the fraud is dependent on which agent is duped by the fraudster. This is described in the following diagram, using the same format as in the case of a direct relationship, discussed above:

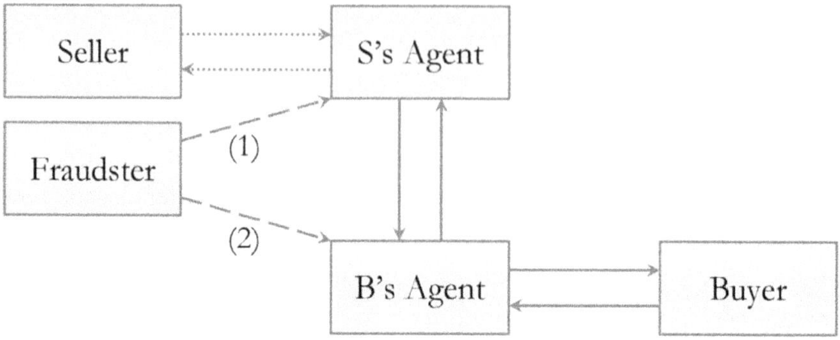

In this example, there are two alternatives, (1) and (2). In (1), the fraudster contacts the seller's agent pretending to be the seller, and therefore excludes the seller from the chain. In (2), the fraudster contacts the buyer's agent pretending to be the seller's agent, and therefore excludes both the seller and the seller's agent from the chain. Once again, the fraudster issues replacement payment instructions, causing the buyer to pay the fraudster.

The question as to which party bears the loss from the fraud closely mirrors the situation where there are no agents at all.

In (1), where the seller's agent is duped, this is equivalent to the situation where the seller's employee wrongfully provides replacement payment details to the buyer. Even if the seller's agent in (1) is not actually authorised to provide the replacement payment instructions, the agent does (subject to any notice that the buyer may have – including pursuant to the parties' contract) have ostensible authority to provide those payment instructions. The seller's agent may also have ostensible authority to communicate to the buyer's agent that the message being communicated did in fact originate with the seller: *cf. First Energy v Hungarian International Bank* [1993] 2 Lloyd's Rep 194 (CA), discussed further below. So in (1), the seller will probably bear the loss of the fraud.

An exception to the general position in respect of (1) would the, perhaps unusual, situation where the seller's agent believes that they are acting in accordance with their authority but the counterparty is on notice that they are not. Consider a situation where an honest seller's agent has been provided with payment instructions which appear to come from the seller, but in truth come from the fraudster. If the seller realises this and notifies the buyer of the potential fraud, it is no answer for the buyer to thereafter pay against the (fraudulent) payment instructions which the buyer receives from the seller's agent. The notice given by the seller is sufficient to contradict the ostensible agency that the seller's agent would otherwise have.

By contrast, (2) is equivalent to the situation where the fraudster uses a confusingly similar email address to contact the buyer directly. The fraudster, in contacting the buyer's agent, has no relevant authority to act for the seller, thus any instructions to the buyer do not bind the seller. The buyer in this case will probably bear the loss of the fraud.

Pure intermediary

The next option is where there is just one intermediary between the parties, but where this intermediary is what is sometimes referred to as a 'pure' intermediary. In other words, the intermediary has no relevant agency functions for the parties, but operates instead simply as a post-box. This is described in the following diagram:

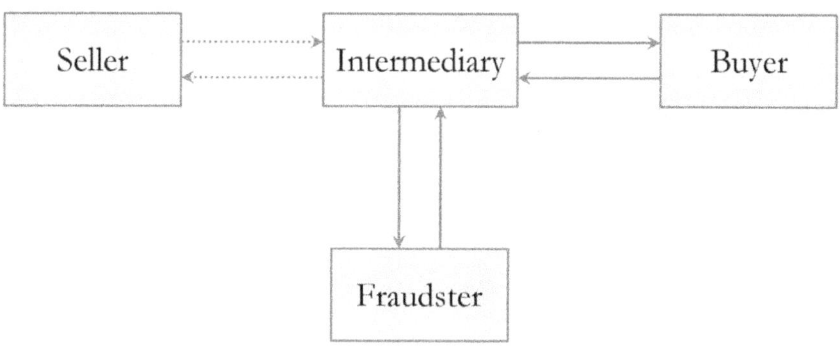

This situation has been considered, albeit strictly *obiter*, in *The Mercedes Envoy* [1995] 2 Lloyd's Rep 559 at 560 per Mance J:

> The originating summons puts forward, as I mentioned, two alternative analyses: firstly, that Howard Houlder were acting for the defendants and, secondly, that they were acting for the plaintiffs. In the event, it seems to me that Howard Houlder were pure intermediaries, that is to say, their only role and authority on behalf of either party was to transmit the communications of the one to the other.
>
> Mr. Gault for the plaintiffs suggested that Howard Houlder might still be clothed with apparent or ostensible authority by each party so that either party would be entitled to treat any actual messages received from Howard Houlder which purported to come from the other party as having actually come from the other party even if they did not do so or did not do so accurately. I do not consider this to be correct. Howard Houlder's only actual authority was to transmit accurately actual messages which they had received. There is no basis on the material before me or in law for treating them as having, or as having been held out as having, any other or wider authority.

The suggestion here is that the pure intermediary had no relevant actual authority – in the case of the fraudulent payment, to pass on payment instructions. Actual authority is limited to accurately transmitting messages received from one party to that party's counterparty. Similarly, the party receiving the message was said not to be entitled to rely on the broker's ostensible authority to confirm that messages transmitted did originate with the recipient's counterparty. This was recently confirmed in *SK Shipping Europe Plc v Capital VLCC 3 Corp* [2021] 2 Lloyd's Rep 109 at [334]-[335] (Foxton J). The limited nature of the duties owed by pure intermediaries was confirmed in *CH Offshore Limited v Internaves Consorcio Naviero SA* [2021] 1 Lloyd's Rep 465 at [68]-[74] (Moulder J).

The buyer in this instance may feel somewhat more aggrieved, given that he could not have discovered the involvement of the fraudster in the chain of communications. However, there are two answers to this objection. First, the buyer has jointly participated in the engagement of the pure intermediary. Second, the intermediary is a mere post-box; the buyer would have not cause to blame a postal delivery service if the buyer received a letter purporting to come from the seller, but actually coming from a fraudster.

However, the question of precisely what authority the pure intermediary has in any given situation is a matter to be determined on the facts and by reference to any relevant contracts (between the counterparties or between either or both of them and the intermediary). In *K v A* [2019] EWHC 1118 (Comm), the court remitted to a tribunal the question of whether receipt by an intermediary broker of bank account details constituted good notice of those details under the parties' contract of sale.

Joint agent – actual agency

The final, and potentially most difficult, variation is where the intermediary is a 'true' agent in that it does have authority to act for both of its principals, the seller and the buyer. This is described in the following diagram:

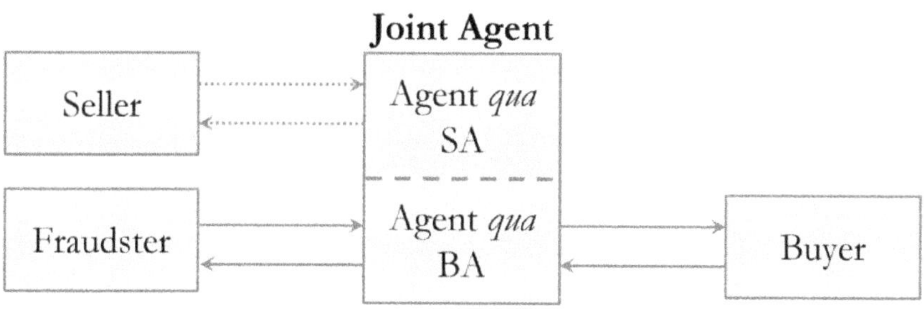

This is perhaps the least frequently-occurring situation, as the joint agent will be in a position where it owes fiduciary duties to competing principals. However, it warrants consideration as there are examples of this form of agency occurring in reported cases (albeit not in the case of cyber fraud): e.g. *RSW International Limited v Purple Surgical Manufacturing Limited* [2022] EWHC 2258 (Comm) at [71] (HHJ Halliwell). Often this variety of joint agency arises where the agent starts out as agent for one party, but by his conduct subsequently takes on agency functions for the other party.

The critical distinction between this situation and the pure intermediary situation, discussed above, is whether or not the intermediary's agency functions include the provision of payment instructions. If so, the joint agent situation applies; if not, the result is the same as if the intermediary was a 'pure' intermediary.

Where the joint agent is the party duped by the fraudster, the question of which principal bears the loss of the fraud is determined by asking for whom was the agent acting when passing the fraudster's message on to the buyer. Was the agent acting as the seller's agent, purporting to provide the buyer with (what the agent believes to be) the seller's payment instructions? Or was the agent acting as the buyer's agent, purporting to tell the principal, the buyer, what the agent (believes it) has been told by the seller?

There is no clear authority which determines this particular issue, though there are some authorities from which the applicable principles may be drawn. These authorities are discussed in detail in McGhee, M. 'Dual capacity brokers, seen through the prism of man-in-the-middle frauds' (2017) 3 LMCLQ 435. This article was considered in *SK Shipping Europe Plc v Capital VLCC 3 Corp* [2021] 2 Lloyd's Rep 109 at [334]-[335]. Foxton J did not adopt this analysis in that case, which concerned pure intermediary agents with authority limited to passing on messages. It is, however, suggested that the analysis remains correct for 'true' joint agency scenarios.

For present purposes, it is sufficient to refer to the following established principles:

(a) Where a joint agent's principals have competing interests, the agent cannot simultaneously act for both. This necessarily follows from the fiduciary duties owed by agents to their principals.

(b) In performing any given act, the joint agent can only be acting for one of the principals: *Emelie Elias v AG of Trinidad & Tobago* [2011] UKPC 19.

(c) Information obtained by the joint agent when acting for one principal is not automatically deemed known to the other principal: *Newsholme Bros v Road Transport & General Insurance* [1929] 2 KB 356.

(d) "*where the two capacities are united in one person, a notice received in one capacity for the purpose of being transmitted to the other is an effectual notice in both capacities.*": *Kingscroft Insurance v Nissan Fire & Marine Insurance* [1999] Lloyd's Rep IR 603, citing *Gale v Lewis* (1846) 9 QB 730.

Drawing these principles together in the situation currently envisaged, the joint agent in communicating (legitimate) payment instructions from the seller to the buyer cannot be simultaneously acting for both buyer and seller. At any given time, by any given act, the agent can only be acting for one of its principals. The authorities contemplate a joint agent may be deemed to receive notice in one capacity (i.e. as agent for one principal) and is then deemed to transmit that notice to the agent's other capacity (i.e. as agent for the other principal). Here, that would be a deemed transmission of the seller's payment instructions as received by the agent from the seller to the agent's other capacity.

Thus, where genuine payment instructions are communicated from the seller to a buyer *via* a joint agent, the agent first receives the instructions from the seller while acting in the agent's capacity as the seller's agent. There is then a deemed transmission of the instruction from the agent (acting for the seller) to itself (acting for the buyer). Practically speaking, nothing physically happens and this deemed transmission follows *scintilla temporis* following the instruction from the seller, but as will be seen this deemed transmission is analytically important. The agent (acting for the buyer) now has knowledge of the instructions and passes them on to the buyer.

Where the agent receives (false) payment instructions from a fraudster, which instructions the agent believes to be coming from the seller, how does this analysis apply? In the case of false instructions, there were *a fortiori* no genuine instructions from the seller, which means that the agent's capacity as the seller's agent is probably not engaged. The agent therefore receives the false instructions solely in its capacity as the buyer's agent. The agent communicates to the buyer the false payment instructions, which the agent believes to have come from the seller (just as, in the direct relationship scenario, the buyer believed that instructions which it received directly from the fraudster were from the seller).

The result of this is that, so far as actual agency is concerned, the joint agent who passes on fraudulent instructions to the buyer is probably acting exclusively for the buyer. Thus, the agent's actions do not bind the seller. A buyer who pays in accordance with the agent's directions is therefore probably required (subject to the following section) to pay the seller (in the buyer's eyes, again; from the seller's perspective, properly).

Joint agent – ostensible agency

In the joint agency situation just discussed, a buyer may legitimately feel aggrieved. The buyer has paid in accordance with the joint agent's instructions, which were said (by the joint agent) to have come from the seller. The buyer had no means of discovering that the instructions did not genuinely come from the seller – that was solely within the gift of the agent. The buyer may have recourse against the agent, as will be explored later. However, the buyer may also have an alternative argument by which he can claim to have discharged his obligations to the seller.

The buyer could argue that the agent had ostensible authority to represent that messages which it, the agent, conveys to the buyer are genuinely from the seller. This may be said to be an application of the rule in *First Energy (UK) Ltd v Hungarian International Bank Ltd* [1993] 2 Lloyd's Rep 194 (CA).

First Energy concerned a facility letter that was negotiated between a company and a bank, with a particular employee of the bank being authorised to negotiate on the bank's behalf but not to make a contractual offer. The facility letter was agreed in principle, but no contract actually concluded. The bank's employee later sent a letter to the company which suggested that the bank had approved and was making a contractual offer capable of immediate acceptance. The company purported to accept the offer.

It was held that the employee was an agent of the bank. The company was aware that the employee did not have actual authority to make a contractual offer, but it was held that the employee nevertheless had ostensible authority to communicate that the bank's head office had made the offer. Evans LJ stated (at 206) that: "*there is clearly no requirement that the authority to communicate decisions should be commensurate with the authority to enter into a transaction of the kind in question on behalf of the principal.*" The bank was accordingly bound by the representation of its agent.

First Energy is often criticised as allowing an agent to pull itself up by its own bootstraps, to clothe itself in agency even when not authorised. However, *First Energy* was approved in *Kelly v Fraser* [2013] 1 AC 450 at [14]-[16] (Lord Sumption JSC).

Applying the reasoning in *First Energy*, the buyer in the situation currently under consideration could argue that, although the agent was not acting with the seller's actual authority (on the analysis above) to provide replacement payment instructions, the agent was generally clothed by the seller with ostensible authority to communicate to the buyer that any particular communication was genuinely from the seller. They buyer could therefore rely on that ostensible authority (to communicate that the, in truth fraudulent, instructions had come from the seller) as against the seller (to discharge the buyer's debt under the contract).

Subject to the ordinary bootstraps caveat about *First Energy* arguments, this argument is attractive in that it reflects the natural sympathy that one might have with the buyer in this situation, who is required to trust that the joint agent will only pass on genuine messages. However, the argument on ostensible authority probably fails for the same reason that the argument on actual authority fails – i.e. the agent is not at any relevant time acting on behalf of the seller when passing on payment instructions which actually originated with a fraudster.

The analysis on actual authority is concerned with establishing for which party an agent is purporting to act at any given time. In accordance with that analysis, where the fraudster passes payment instructions to the buyer through the agent, the agent is not at any point acting on behalf of the seller. There is no reason why this same analysis should not apply equally to both actual acts of agency and implicit representations made by the agent. Thus, the agent's capacity as the seller's agent is never engaged, so the agent never represents that the relevant message has been received from the seller.

Even if the principles in *First Energy* could be said to be *prima facie* applicable, it may be that the nature of the joint agent's message is sufficient to put the buyer on inquiry and thus displace any (reasonable) reliance on the ostensible authority. In *Stavrinides v Bank of Cyprus* [2019] EWHC 1328 (Ch), John Kimbell QC explained that in *First Bank* it was unrealistic to suggest that the company ought to have checked with the bank, notwithstanding the employee's letter. The judge stated (at [103]) that "*the more usual the transaction, the more likely it is that it will be held that the contractor is put on notice that the agent may lack authority.*" It may be argued that an unexpected change in payment instructions, particularly in industries where such frauds are relatively well-known, is sufficiently unusual to put the buyer on notice.

Action against banks

This section will consider the position of a buyer who has mistakenly paid a fraudster, as discussed in the example above, but is still liable to pay the seller. It will discuss how the buyer might seek to recover its loss from parties other than the fraudster.

Often parties in the position of the buyer look to the banking chain, banks both being the obvious next step, and having deep pockets from which to satisfy a claim for damages. Notwithstanding this natural inclination, consideration should also be given to which other third parties may be held liable instead of or in addition to banks. These other third parties will be addressed in the following section.

The buyer will most naturally seek to recover from third parties the sum which was mistakenly paid to the fraudster. However, if the third party is liable in damages, then the buyer may well be able to claim other losses consequent on the fraud. Subject to ordinary principles of damages, such as mitigation, the buyer may be able to claim similar losses from the third parties as it can claim from the fraudster directly.

This section considers the claims that the victim might have in law. However, regard may also be had to whether there are other means of recourse – such as against banks under the Contingent Reimbursement Model Code or through the Financial Ombudsman Service.

Notably, the ombudsman has been empowered to consider complaints made by victims about the conduct of receiving banks since January 2019, as well as the victim's own bank. The ombudsman is empowered to make awards of up to £375,000 against individual regulated firms, which awards are binding if formally accepted by the complainant. This is an effective alternative means by which a victim can pursue redress. The ombudsman will take into account the law, codes and good practice that applied at the time of the event, but is not bound to apply those matters strictly and will decide the complaint on a fair and reasonable basis. A recent review of ombudsman decisions against both remitting and receiving banks suggests that the ombudsman takes a more generous approach to compensating victims: Leow, R. 'Recovering mistaken payments before the Financial Ombudsman' (2019) 2 LMCLQ 216.

Victim's bank

Breach of mandate

Where a claim is required, the first and most natural port of call for a victim to consider is the terms of its contract with its bank. The banking contract will establish the framework of the relationship between the victim and its bank, and will in particular identify the terms on which the bank is both entitled and obliged to make payments from the victim's account – i.e. the bank's mandate.

The most straightforward claim that a victim of cyber fraud can make is one for breach of mandate. Where a bank makes a payment out of a customer's account without authority then it is treated as though the bank made those payments out of its own funds, rather than the customer's. If the victim can demonstrate that the payments were not authorised under the banking contract, then the victim can seek a declaration to reverse the debits on its account and may also be able to claim for further losses suffered as a result of the fraud.

This would be straightforward claim that could be made where the bank paid against instructions received from a confusingly similar email address to that of the authorised signatory on the account. It would be more complicated where the actual email address of the signatory had been compromised. If the banking contract, on its proper construction, required that the person whose address it was actually authorised the relevant transactions, it would not be sufficient for the bank to rely on an email received (unwittingly) from a fraudster who had sent it from the address of the authorised signatory. As explained above, the authority is that of the person not of the email address. However, if the bank's mandate was to pay against banking instructions communicated from a particular email address, the mandate being silent as to the identity of the person operating that address, there probably would not be a breach of mandate if the bank paid against the fraudulent instructions in these circumstances.

Quincecare *duty*

In addition to their express contractual duties, banks are also subject to the *Quincecare* duty of care – an implied contractual duty to exercise reasonable care and skill, coupled with a co-extensive duty of care in tort. In *Barclays Bank Plc v Quincecare Ltd* [1992] 4 All ER 363, Steyn J identified that there is

> a duty on a bank to refrain from executing a customer's order if, and for so long as, the bank is 'put on inquiry' in the sense that the bank has reasonable grounds for believing—assessed according to the standards of an ordinary prudent banker—that the order is an attempt to defraud the customer

The *Quincecare* duty was confirmed in *Singularis Holdings Ltd v Daiwa Capital Markets Europe Ltd* [2019] UKSC 50, being the first occasion (and, other than a single DIFC case discussed below, the only occasion) that damages were awarded for breach of the *Quincecare* duty. The decision in *Singularis* also made clear that the duty still applied, and the bank could still be liable to the customer, even where the impugned order was made by the controlling mind and will of the company, such as in a single director organisation.

The *Quincecare* duty was also discussed in *JP Morgan v Nigeria* [2019] EWCA Civ 1641, which also considered the effect of various contractual provisions in the banking contract which the bank claimed to have the effect of excluding or limiting the *Quincecare* duty. The Court of Appeal confirmed that the *Quincecare* duty is "*inherent*" in the banking relationship and, while "*not impossible*" to contract out of, can only be excluded by "*clear*" wording.

JP Morgan also explained in further detail what the *Quincecare* duty required of a bank. In *Quincecare* itself, the duty was said to be one not to make the impugned payment. However, the court in *JP Morgan* indicated that the precise steps which a bank is required to take when put on inquiry – in particular, what duty it is under to check the validity of the transaction, and with whom and how that check should be made – will vary according to the specific facts of each case. However, it seems unlikely that the duty is a purely negative one not to make payment.

There have since been a number of cases addressing the *Quincecare* duty. These are reviewed in McGhee, M. & Kennedy, M. 'Different jurisdictions' approaches to Quincecare: England and Wales lead the expansive approach' (2022) 10 JIBFL 674. The key developments have been as follows:

First, the duty is engaged where a customer in fact authorised the transaction: *Philipp v Barclays Bank* [2022] QB 578 (CA) (under appeal). It therefore extends to natural person customers, not just corporate customers. Previously, there were suggestions that the duty was concerned with the bank preventing a fraud being perpetrated on the company by an agent.

Second, the duty is limited to the bank's customer. It does not extend to the creditors of that customer (*Stanford International Bank v HSBC* [2021] 1 WLR 3507 (CA), upheld on appeal) or to victims of fraud who pay money into the customer's account (*RBS v JP SPC 4* [2022] UKPC 18).

Third, the duty is owed by banks, but the question of what (if any) other financial entities might owe the equivalent duty remains unexplored. *Hamblin v World First* [2020] EWHC 2383 (Comm) concerned allegations that the duty was owed by an e-money institution providing international payment services, but without the existence or content of that duty being ruled on. It is open to argument that, for example, a suitably-organised crypto-exchange could owe a *Quincecare* (or analogous) duty. If so, there is an open question as to whether a non-bank is to be held to the standard of a 'prudent banker' or whether it should be, for example, the standard of a 'prudent exchange'.

Fourth, the matters which will put an entity on inquiry, sufficient to engage the duty, will vary from case to case. However, the matters must be specific to the impugned transaction, not the customer generally: *Nigeria v JP Morgan Chase Bank* [2022] EWHC 1447 (Comm). As Birss LJ explained in *Philipp* at [60], "*The key is the careful calibration of the Quincecare duty itself. It is a duty conditioned by whatever ordinary banking practice is at the relevant time.*" The precise content of standard banking practice is a matter open for evidence in each case: e.g. *Tecnimont Arabia v NatWest* [2022] EWHC 1172 (Comm) at [161(c)] (HHJ Bird).

In *Aegis Resources DMCC v Union Bank of India* [2020] DIFC CFI 004, the DIFC court found that a bank was in breach of mandate when making a payment because the instruction to do so had come from a fraudster instead of the account holder. The court then went on to find that this was also a breach of the bank's *Quincecare* duty. This is somewhat inconsistent, given that the duty to exercise reasonable care and skill in executing the customer's orders is not engaged where the bank is in breach of mandate for making a payment not in accordance with the customer's orders. The court explained that the bank ought to have been put on enquiry by reason of the fact that a new beneficiary was being paid, the payment instructions were only sent by email (normally being additionally conveyed by fax or phone call) and the purported supporting invoice did not identify a specific invoice number in the usual format. These matters are relatively minor in the scheme of cyber frauds, so it is likely that the decision will be confined to its facts on this point.

For completeness, it is possible that the bank might also close the victim's account out of a concern that the account was being used for fraudulent purposes (albeit potentially without the customer's knowledge). The customer might have a claim against their bank in these circumstances for breach of contract, as discussed in *N v Royal Bank of Scotland* [2019] EWHC 1770 (Comm) and *R (TF Global Markets (UK) (trading as ThinkMarkets)) v Financial Ombudsman Service Limited* [2020] EWHC 3178 (Admin).

Fraudster's bank

Reference here is made to the 'fraudster's bank' as a convenient shorthand for the account into which the fraudulent proceeds are received (whether initially, from the victim's account, or at subsequent remove). Sometimes this account is set up by the fraudster or its agents for use in fraud, or sometimes it is the fraudster's bank account used in the fraudster's normal, non-fraudulent operations (the former is more common where the fraud or frauds is or are perpetrated on a large scale).

However, this account can also be the account of third parties to the fraud. These third parties may be willing providers of their bank account to the fraudsters, often in exchange for payment. These third parties (sometimes referred to as 'money mules'), may not have actual knowledge of what the fraudster is doing, though a reasonable inference is that would involve money laundering and the 'money mules' ought to have known that. Alternatively, rather than being willing providers, the third parties may have themselves been the subject of a cyber fraud or other attack by the fraudster, who thereby gained access to the account without the consent (or perhaps even knowledge) of the account holder.

The principal difficulty for the victim is that (almost invariably) it had no prior and relevant relationship or contact with the fraudster's bank before the fraud took place. Therefore, the fraudster's bank did not owe any duties to the specific victim of the fraud. The victim's relationship with the fraudster's bank, prior to any fraud, was no different to that bank's relationship with any other person, company or entity in the world.

In particular, unlike with their own bank, the victim did not have a contractual relationship with the fraudster's bank. As confirmed in *RBS v JP SPC 4* [2022] UKPC 1 at [57]-[58] (see also *Tulip Trading Limited v Bitcoin Association for BSV* [2022] EWHC 667 (Ch) at [103]), this will be fatal to any attempt to impose a *Quincecare* or similar duty on the fraudster's bank.

There are 4 further options available (see McGhee, M. 'Orthodoxy prevails? How banks avoid liability for their customers' frauds' (2022) 6 JIBFL 450):-

Restitution for unjust enrichment

The essence of the victim's argument is that when a bank receives a payment in respect of a particular customer's account, the funds become part of the bank's general stock of assets and the customer is merely entitled in debt to a payment from the bank equivalent to the funds credited. The bank is accordingly enriched and is liable in unjust enrichment to give restitution to the victim in respect of the sums fraudulently misappropriated from the victim's account and deposited with the fraudster's bank. The bank's response is typically that it is the customer, not the bank, which is in truth enriched and against whom any claim for restitution lies; alternatively, the bank raises the defences of ministerial receipt and change of position.

The question of enrichment is a live issue in the law, and one which the courts have expressly stated is not suitable for summary judgment given the potentially conflicting approaches expressed by the authorities and degree to which their application is necessarily fact-specific: *High Commissioner for Pakistan v Prince Mukkaram* [2016] EWHC 1465 at [140]-[150] (Henderson J) and *Marsfield Automotive Inc v Siddiqi* [2017] EWHC 187 (Comm) at [27]-[36] (Teare J).

In favour of the position which a victim might take, in *Jones v Churcher* [2009] EWHC 722 (QB) a bank was held liable in unjust enrichment in respect of withdrawals made by the bank's customer after the bank had been given notice of the fact that the payment into the customer's account with the bank had been made by mistake. However, in the subsequent case of *Jeremy D Stone Consultants Ltd v National Westminster Bank Plc* [2013] EWHC 206 (Ch), it was held (without apparent reference to *Jones*) that a bank was not enriched (alternatively could avail itself of the defence of ministerial receipt) because the bank received the payments for its customer and was immediately obliged to credit the sums to the customer's accounts, and because the bank had no entitlement to refuse withdrawals by the customer of those sums.

This is an area which will benefit from a careful and authoritative ruling in due course, ideally from an appellate court. In addition to the conflicting authority on the point, there are broader arguments of principle or theoretical basis which weigh on the point.

In favour of holding a bank liable in unjust enrichment, it may be observed that the historic authorities against that proposition do not reflect modern commercial practice. For example, it was previously said that banks should not be required to play "*amateur detective*" and subject an account's activity to "*microscopic examination*": *Lloyds Bank v The Chartered Bank of India, Australia and China* [1929] 1 KB 40 (Sankey LJ). However, in the 90 years since that decision, modern banking technologies have become available which allow accounts to be subject to that form of examination on a semi-automatic basis. Further, the regulatory obligations on banks now include extensive anti-money laundering and know-your-client checks which do require a bank to act as a detective, scrutinising their customers' assertions.

Equally, it might be said that it would be wrong to find banks liable in unjust enrichment for their receipt of funds on behalf of their customers precisely because the banks are merely providing a service to their customers. If given the option, on any sensible view the party which is 'truly' enriched is the bank's customer. This would certainly be the case if the bank received and stored in the customer's vault physical coins. The mere fact that modern banking operates as a series of debits and credits on inter-bank debt ledgers should not change the underlying principle that a bank merely receives money as the agent of the customer.

As to the defences of ministerial receipt and change of position, a crucial issue is the degree of knowledge of the bank as the person relying on the defence. If a bank is on notice of the relevant facts, they may be deprived of any defence they might otherwise have if they then allow the funds to be dissipated.

Putting the bank on notice

The most obvious means by which the receiving bank is put on notice, such that they are for example deprived of a defence of change of position, is if the bank is given actual notice. Thus, a receiving bank is likely to be on notice where it allows funds to be dissipated notwithstanding the payor providing timeous notice to the bank that the payment was induced by a fraud. However, most cases of notice are not this straightforward.

In *Niru Battery v Milestone* [2002] EWHC 1425 (Comm) at [135], Moore-Bick J considered the extent of notice required and suggested that the matter was a question of good faith. The judge explained that bad faith:

> "is capable of embracing a failure to act in a commercially acceptable way and sharp practice of a kind that falls short of outright dishonesty as well as dishonesty itself. The factors which will determine whether it is inequitable to allow the claimant to obtain restitution in a case of mistaken payment will vary from case to case"

The judge went on to suggest that the difficult case was one "*where the payee has grounds for believing that the payment may have been made by mistake, but cannot be sure. In such cases good faith may well dictate that an enquiry be made of the payer.*": at [135].

The language of commercial acceptability echoes *Cowan de Groot Properties Ltd v Eagle Trust plc* [1992] 4 All ER 700 at 761, where Knox J held that:

> "In my judgment it may well be that the underlying broad principle which runs through the authorities regarding commercial transactions is that the court will impute knowledge, on the basis of what a reasonable person would have learnt, to a person who is guilty of commercially unacceptable conduct in the particular context involved."

It has since been held that a conscious decision not to follow KYC procedures can give rise to 'blind eye' knowledge of matters that would have been identified by those procedures: *Armstrong DLW GmbH v Winnington Networks Ltd* [2013] Ch 156 at [278]-[279] (Stephen Morris QC).

In a slightly different context, it has been held that a bank has constructive notice of a transaction's impropriety where the bank gave insufficient consideration to the commercial purpose of the transaction: *Papadimitriou v Crédit Agricole* [2015] 1 WLR 4265 (PC). Lord Sumption JSC explained (at [33]):

> "if there are features of the transaction such that if left unexplained they are indicative of wrongdoing, then an explanation must be sought before it can be assumed that there is none. In the present case, on the facts actually known to the bank, there was no apparent explanation of the interposition of the Panamanian and Liechtenstein entities unless it was to conceal the origin of funds derived from third parties. That was why the bank had to make inquiries before proceeding as if there was an innocent explanation."

Precisely what is required effectively to put the bank on inquiry will vary from case to case. Examples might include a significant change in their customer's payment practices, such as transacting in new currencies, new jurisdictions, or in unusually large sums. Indeed, a sudden slew of transactions on a previously-dormant account might be such a change. There is room to consider the extent to which a bank should be put on notice where the activity of its customer did not match the customer's indications in account opening documentation as to the account's expected usage: compare *I.F.T. S.A.L. Offshore v Barclays Bank Plc* [2020] EWHC 3125 (Comm) at [10] & [14] with *Tecnimont Arabia Limited v National Westminster Bank plc* [2022] EWHC 1172 (Comm) at [55].

Where a bank fails to respond to or overrides any internal systems it has for identifying suspicious activity, that might also provide a basis for imputing constructive notice to the bank. More difficult issues might arise where reliance is placed on the bank's internal systems being so inadequate that they failed to identify a suspicious transaction, or where the bank's system has issued an alert about an incoming payment for manual review, but only a relatively short time after that (and before the alert has been reviewed) the incoming payment is then paid out to a third party. These more difficult situations should be considered against the touchstone whether a reasonable, honest banker would have acted the same or whether the receiving bank was guilty of 'commercially unacceptable conduct'.

That said, it is important not to elide the issue of what is of 'commercially unacceptable conduct' and what the claimant asserts to be a 'commercially unacceptable outcome'. That may be where the claimant in *Stanford International Bank (in liquidation) v HSBC* [2021] 1 WLR 3507 (CA) (upheld on appeal) went into error. There, as discussed in the earlier section on dishonest assistance, the claimant started from the position that transactions were made which ought not to have been made, such that the defendant bank's operations as a whole were to be characterised as dishonest. However, the claim was struck out because the claimant did not identify what actions, by whom, constituted 'commercially unacceptable conduct' and why the bank should be held responsible for those actions.

There is scope to draw comparisons between matters which will give rise to constructive notice on the part of a receiving bank with the sort of matters which will trigger the sending bank's *Quincecare* duty (discussed above). Thus, it might be thought that mere suspicion – including general suspicion about the customer – is unlikely to be sufficient, by analogy with *Nigeria v JP Morgan Chase Bank* [2022] EWHC 1447 (Comm). There should be something specific relating to the transaction which is being impugned in order to put the receiving bank on inquiry. However, it seems that a receiving bank may be held to a stricter standard; in *Abou-Rahmah v Abacha* [2007] 1 Lloyd's Rep 115 at [50]-[52], Rix LJ held that "*It is not commercially acceptable for banks who suspect "in a general way" would-be customers of being involved in money laundering to open up accounts for them.*" The judge continued at [55]:

> "I have nevertheless concluded that if a bank opens an account for suspected money launderers and nevertheless is justified in saying to defrauded claimants who seek restitution that it is entitled to make good a defence of change of position in the absence of knowledge or suspicions about individual transactions, then the international concern with the vice of money laundering is not being taken seriously, and I fear will not be taken seriously."

Accessorial liability – dishonest assistance or knowing receipt

Assuming that the victim can make out a proprietary claim over the sums paid to the fraudster's bank, the victim can seek to make the fraudster's bank liable as an accessory to the customer's breach of trust, whether as a dishonest assistant of a breach of trust (i.e. the subsequent dissipation of the trust fund) or as an unconscionable recipient of the trust funds.

For the purpose of a dishonest assistance claim, as discussed above, the bank is required to do no more than assist its customers breach of trust in a way which is of more than minimal importance. That is unlikely to be the key issue. The more problematic matter will be providing the requisite 'dishonesty'. This will engage very similar analysis to that in the previous sub-section regarding what will put a receiving bank on notice of wrongdoing.

As to 'knowing' receipt, there are two matters which will need to be addressed. First, the issue of whether the bank or the bank's customer received the funds for their own benefit. In this regard, see the discussion above as to whether the fraudster's bank is (unjustly) enriched in these circumstances. Second, the claimant must establish that the bank defendant had sufficient knowledge "*to render it unconscionable for him to retain the benefit of the receipt*": *BCCI v Akindele* [2001] Ch 437 at 455 (Nourse LJ). That, again, will canvass very similar territory to whether the bank was 'dishonest'.

Novel duty of care in tort

The victim can seek to establish a novel duty of care in tort, distinct from the novel duty argued for in *JP SPC 4*. There are, unarguably, difficulties in establishing both the existence and the content of such a duty.

In *Customs and Excise Commissioners v Barclays Bank Plc* [2007] 1 AC 181, the House of Lords was concerned with whether a bank, with notice of a freezing injunction over the account of the bank's customer, owed a duty of care to the third party who had applied for the freezing injunction and maintained a substantial claim against the banks customer. The court held that the bank owed no duty to the third party to take reasonable care to comply with the injunction.

In determining the scope of the bank's duty, the court considered both the *Caparo* three-stage test (foreseeability of damage, proximity between parties, and whether imposing a duty would be fair just and reasonable) and the assumption of responsibility test. The court also considered the need to take care only to extend the existing law incrementally. Applying those tests to this new alleged duty of care, the bank and the third party were not in a proximate relationship and the bank had not assumed any responsibility to the third party.

It is arguable that in cases of fraud, where a proprietary claim is made to the frozen assets and the bank is notified of the fraud or the proprietary claim, the position may be different. In such cases, the victim has a direct interest in the assets held by the fraudster's bank. The bank is therefore more likely to owe a duty to the victim not to allow the assets to be dissipated. This is on the basis that the bank holds the victim's property, and thus that there is a more proximate relationship between the parties.

However, the issue will be whether it would be fair, just and reasonable to impose that duty on the bank which may conflict with the bank's *prima facie* duty to its client to follow legitimate payment instructions. The tension between these duties is more significant than the equivalent tension in the *Quincecare* situation because the tension here is between different duties said to be owed to different persons, whereas the duties in the *Quincecare* situation are both owed to the same person (the customer). Any duty to the victim in this instance would likely be limited to cases where the bank was at least permitted by its contractual terms and regulatory obligations to freeze its customer's account. It is also relevant to consider the fact that any given bank will have a "*huge number of potential payers who can remit monies without significant control by the bank*", such that "*The imposition of a duty of care in relation to such persons (in the absence of special circumstances) would in practice impose very heavy burdens on banks and significantly hamper their efficiency.*": *Abou-Rahmah v Abacha* [2005] EWHC 2662 (QB) at [68] (Treacy J).

Against this background, a victim of fraud will probably have to identify some fault in the fraudster's bank's processes after the bank received notice of the fraud or the victim's proprietary claim.

It is hard to conceive of a claim that the victim might have any earlier than this. For example, the victim may consider that the receiving bank failed to take reasonable care to scrutinise the account opening and KYC information provided by the bank's (fraudulent) customer, thus enabling the fraudster to open an account under a false name or a false identity (including contact details). The bank's failings when opening the account may have provided the opportunity for the claimant loss – such as by limiting the claimant's ability to identify and pursue the wrongdoer. However, at the time of any such failings, there was nothing to distinguish the claimant (who was at that time not a victim of fraud) from any other person in the world.

However, these earlier actions predated any conceivable connection between the victim and the bank. It is therefore difficult to establish the necessary proximity or assumption of responsibility to make the fraudster's bank liable in tort to the victim in respect of any loss that may be said to have been suffered by the victim as the result of these failures: *cf. P&P Property Ltd v Owen White & Catlin LLP* [2019] Ch 273 (CA) at [81]-[82] (Patten LJ) (conveyancers owed no duty of care to client's counterparty to properly conduct identity checks on the client).

Alternatively, it may be said that the bank has a relationship (of sorts) with the victim following receipt of the victim's funds. Criticisms may then be made that the bank may have failed to take reasonable care in monitoring activity on its customer's account – for example, by allowing substantial international payments to be received into and quickly dissipated from an account which ordinarily processed only small domestic transactions. However, it is hard to see how a duty of care to the victim arises in these circumstances, particularly following the decision in *JP SPC 4*. It is probably not enough for a bank to become aware of a suspicious transaction, and consider that it is the proceeds of a fraud 'a' victim, if the bank was not aware of it being a fraud on the specific victim claimant: *Hill v Chief Constable of West Yorkshire* [1989] AC 53. Hence why notification by the victim to the receiving bank is the most likely transition point.

There is evidence that banks have been less prompt in responding to notices of fraud than they ought to be. In a report published in November 2019, Economic Crime: Consumer View, the Treasury Committee recorded its concerns:

> over the length of time some accounts used in economic crime remain active once intelligence has been received on their potential misuse. … We recommend that the FCA should set a challenging timeframe in which an account must be frozen when evidence has been received by a bank that it is receiving money fraudulently. We understand the argument made by the FCA that a timeframe may encourage financial firms to work towards the prescribed timeframe, rather than as quickly as possible, but without a deadline, some accounts are remaining open for weeks allowing further fraud to occur unnecessarily.

If a duty could be established to the victim of fraud, what actions by a bank would constitute breach of that duty? An obvious example might include where the bank then permits subsequent dissipation of traceable proceeds of the fraud which remained in the account at the time of the notification. However, a court considering this point would have regard to the bank's contractual and regulatory obligations in this context, including under any non-English local law obligations. The bank will be given a reasonable period to respond to the notification procedure.

Action against other third parties

Banks are not the only potential target for the victim of a fraud. Other third parties who have been or became involved in the transaction could also have liability to the victim.

Agent

For the purposes of this section, 'agent' includes both actually authorised agents and pure intermediaries, as discussed above in the context of actions against a counterparty.

If a buyer has been the victim of a fraud where the fraudster successfully tricked the buyer's agent into believing that replacement payment instructions from the fraudster were in fact from the seller, for the reasons above it is unlikely that the buyer can escape liability to pay the seller (from the buyer's perspective, again). However, the buyer may then seek to claim against the agent whose susceptibility to the fraud exposed the buyer to the loss which eventuated.

Frequently, the relationship between the buyer and the agent will be covered by an express contract agreed between the parties. The terms of this contract will be the first port of call as they may expressly provide for certain obligations or limitations which apply to this situation.

Alternatively, if there is no express contract agreed, it is likely that an implied contract can be identified. If the agent is being remunerated for providing the agency services, this ought not to be difficult. Where there is an understanding or obligation (including pursuant to the Commercial Agents (Council Directive) Regulations 1993) that the agent will receive some consideration from the buyer in exchange for providing agency services, the law will readily imply a contract. Again, the terms of that implied contract may make provision for situations such as the one presently envisaged.

The buyer will also wish to consider the term implied by s.13 Supply of Goods and Services Act 1982. Given increasing prevalence of frauds such as those discussed in this text, there is a very creditable argument that 'reasonable skill and care' would include checking the email addresses which apparently genuine instructions are sent from. This argument is all the stronger where the agent acts as a professional agent, with the law holding such individuals to a higher standard. It might similarly be argued that an agent exercising reasonable skill and care would be expected to be alert to certain 'red flag' instructions, such as changes to payment instructions (especially to accounts in different names, with different banks or in different jurisdictions).

If it can be established that an agent's obligation to exercise reasonable skill and care requires the agent to respond to situations such as these, the question then is what is the minimum standard to which the agent is required to perform. Naturally, this is a reflection of what is reasonable for that agent, acting for that principal, and in those circumstances. However, assuming that the agent is under an obligation to identify and respond to potential frauds such as replacement payment instructions, it is likely that the agent would be required to confirm with its principal whether or not the instructions were legitimate. Given that the potential fraud is, as is commonly the case likely to be perpetrated by email, it is reasonable to expect that the agent would confirm the instructions by some other means of communication (e.g. by telephone).

Another facet of the obligation to supply services with reasonable skill and care is whether that obligation can apply to more passive, or less direct, acts of the agent. So an agent whose role is to pass messages between two parties might be required, by the duty to exercise reasonable care and skill in providing its services, to maintain reasonable cyber security. Again, the question becomes what is 'reasonable' in all the circumstances of the relationship (including by reference to any express terms of the contract). An ordinary commodities broker would probably not be required to have a near-impregnable cyber security system, but that broker might well be required to make use of appropriate and up-to-date security software and to provide some form of appropriate cyber security training to its staff (such as in the identification of red flag messages, or in protecting the broker's system from email phishing attacks).

A specific difficulty that may be encountered in bringing an action against an agent is in proving a causal link between any breach of contract by the agent and any loss caused by the fraud. This may be a particular hurdle where, for example, the agent's failure to use up-to-date software is concerned. Just because the agent did not use up-to-date software and subsequently had its systems compromised by a fraudster does not automatically mean that the buyer can claim its loss from the agent. If the same result would have followed even if the agent's system had been up-to-date, then the agent's breach did not cause the buyer any actionable loss.

Insofar as a contractual duty cannot be alleged for some reason (such as in the unlikely situation of a gratuitous agent), it is likely that the agent would owe a similar (though perhaps somewhat less stringent) duty of care in the tort of negligence. This would be on the basis that there was an assumption of responsibility on the part of the agent for the affairs of the principal.

It might also be possible to frame the claim as a breach of the agent's fiduciary duty, though this would require the agent to have an awareness of the fraud itself. This is because the agent's fiduciary duties only require good faith and loyalty on the part of the agent, not competence. So an incompetent but unwitting agent may be liable in contract or tort, but will not be liable in equity for breach of fiduciary duty. To be liable in equity, the agent would probably have to fail in its duties to the principal, either by acting in bad faith or by preferring the fiduciary's own interests over those of the principal (such as where the agent was in fact party to the fraud).

Other receiving parties

Where the victim of a cyber fraud can identify that funds received beneficially by a third party represent the traceable proceeds of the fraud perpetrated against the victim, the victim will likely want to recover those traceable proceeds directly. In determining whether the victim can claim against the third party, two questions need to be asked: First, does or did the third party have some knowledge of the fraud? Second, did the third party receive the funds as a volunteer or for good consideration?

Turning to the first question, if the third party had some knowledge of the fraud, or merely the fact that the party from whom the third party received the property was not free to dispose of the relevant property unencumbered, it is likely that the third party will be liable as a fraudster. The ways in which a victim might seek to claim against such a third party are discussed above. In particular, a third party recipient at some stages removed from the initial fraudulent transfer is likely to be receiving the payment as a money launderer, or alternatively as an end beneficiary of the fraud or by way of remuneration for that party's participation in the fraud (for example, by compromising the victim's bank account). In these circumstances, the recipient may be liable in knowing receipt, dishonest assistance, unlawful means conspiracy or unjust enrichment.

In the case of an innocent third-party recipient, with no knowledge of the fraud or the tainted nature of the funds, whether or not the victim has a claim depends on whether the third party received the funds as a volunteer or for payment. In the case of a gratuitous recipient, their innocent receipt alone cannot defeat any proprietary claim that the victim may have to the funds. It is also possible that the victim could make a claim in unjust enrichment against the third-party recipient, subject to meeting the *Investment Trust* criteria for indirect recipients.

If, however, the innocent third party received the traceable proceeds for good consideration, it is unlikely that the victim will be able to bring a claim against them. So the party who receives the victim's money (or the traceable proceeds of the fraud) in discharge of a debt owed (for example, arising under a contract for the sale of goods) will be entitled to retain the funds that it has received.

Person from whom fraudster obtained data

This category of third party is concerned with how the fraudster identified the opportunity to perpetrate the cyber fraud. Many cyber frauds are simply targeted at any individual without any background knowledge, but in some cases (such as interference with existing contracts) the fraud depends on the fraudster having already acquired some information, or data, which is necessary to perpetrate the fraud. This section addresses whether the victim of a fraud can bring a claim in respect of the fraud against the fraudster's data source.

It may be that the data source was in fact the victim. For example, the fraudster might have compromised the victim's email server directly and thus become privy to the victim's existing business and its operational procedures. However, in other cases the fraudster might have obtained data from other persons, to whom the victim might look for compensation.

Counterparty as the source of the data

It may be that the fraudster has been able to perpetrate the fraud on the victim because the fraudster has compromised the systems of the victim's counterparty.

Consider a buyer who receives an invoice on the seller's standard form which instructs the buyer to make payment to a particular account, but where that account subsequently transpires to be the account of a fraudster who obtained the invoice template by compromising the seller's computer systems. The seller may well be at fault for maintaining inadequate cybersecurity. If so, this has arguably led to the fraudster obtaining access to the seller's emails and thereby causing loss to the buyer (assuming that the buyer is liable to pay again). The aggrieved buyer might want to hold the seller legally responsible for the fraud, notwithstanding that (for the reasons explained above) the buyer remains *prima facie* liable to pay the seller the contract price.

The first question to be asked is whether the seller's fault constitutes an actionable breach of a duty owed to the buyer.

It may be that there is a term of the parties' contract which the buyer can claim to have been breached by the seller, though express terms dealing with matters such as cyber security are not yet commonplace in most contracts. It is at least possible that some commonly included terms of contracts which oblige the parties to keep the terms of the contract private and confidential might be available for the buyer to rely on. For example, if the seller disposes of printed copies of the contract and inter party correspondence in a non-secure manner and this permits the fraudster to identify the opportunity, it may be that the buyer can claim that this was a breach of contract. That said, it is unlikely that the parties intended the pertinent term to cover these sorts of situations.

Any given case will turn on the precise wording of the contract. Regard may also be had to any necessary implied terms of the contract, though the court is careful to ensure that terms are implied only in proper instances.

Sell Your Car With Us Ltd v Sareen [2019] EWHC 2332 (Ch) concerned a case where A sold B's car for B and was liable under the parties' contract to pay the sale price to B. B provided account details by email and directed A to make payment to that account. The fraudster then sent A an email from an address, which was confusingly similar to B's, and instructed A to pay a different account. A sought to call B to confirm the change, but failed to make the connection. The fraudster then called A to confirm the (fraudulent) details. A then made payment.

In that case, A argued that it was an implied term of the contract with B that B would take reasonable care over the security of his email communications. If B failed to take reasonable care, thereby enabling a fraudster to access the communications, B was precluded by his own breach from suing A for the agreed sum. ICC Judge Burton in *Sareen* dismissed the argument, finding there to be no need for the implied term so as to give the contract business efficacy. It was not relevant that the contract would have been improved by the implied term: *Ali v Petroleum Co of Trinidad and Tobago* [2017] UKPC 2.

To similar effect, an attempt to amend a claim in analogous circumstances, relying on an alleged implied contractual duty to take reasonable care in maintaining cyber-security, failed in *Rijksmuseum Twenthe v Simon C Dickinson Ltd* (unreported, 30 January 2020).

Instead of contract, the buyer could seek to formulate an actionable breach in tort. The difficulty is in formulating a duty of care which the seller owed specifically to the buyer. Even if the seller negligently failed to follow good practice in maintaining a minimum expected standard of cyber security, it is not clear that the seller owed a duty to the buyer to act otherwise. In the absence of a specific duty owed by the seller to the buyer, any fault of the seller is not legally relevant.

The exception to this would be where the counterparty can be held responsible for their omission (e.g. to maintain adequate cyber security) by reason of one of the situations identified by Lord Goff in *Smith v Littlewoods Organisation* [1987] AC 241. The more straightforward way of establishing this would be where there is an assumption of responsibility on the part of the counterparty which can be said to extend to maintaining adequate cyber security. For example, if the seller invited the buyer to use a particular secure messaging platform but then failed to ensure that the platform was appropriately secured, this may be sufficient to allow the buyer to allege a breach by the seller in the event of fraudulent interference with the platform.

In *Rijksmuseum Twenthe v Simon C Dickinson Ltd* (unreported, 30 January 2020), the court dismissed the suggestion that (on the facts as alleged) there could be a novel duty of care owed by the seller to its counterparty in negotiations to protect the buyer from suffering pure economic loss (i.e. in paying the price twice). HHJ Pelling QC explained (with reference to *Greenway v Johnson Matthey* [2016] EWCA 408 and *Playboy Club v BNL SPA* [2018] UKSC 43) that for such a duty to exist in any given case, the seller must be shown to have voluntarily assumed responsibility for the envisaged loss and that the buyer relied on that assumption of responsibility.

The more difficult alternative would be to argue that the seller "*negligently causes or permits to be created a source of danger, and it is reasonably foreseeable that third parties may interfere with it and, sparking off the danger, thereby cause damage to persons in the position of the [buyer]*": *Smith* at 272. Arguably, a failure to maintain appropriate cyber security standards negligently causes a source of danger, and it is similarly arguable that third party fraudsters may exploit that source of danger. The question is whether it would also be reasonably foreseeable that interference by the fraudsters would cause the buyer to suffer loss. This may be a more difficult argument to make, certainly in the abstract, as it is contingent on the interaction between the fraudster and the buyer.

Assuming that the buyer can identify an actionable breach, the second question is as to the consequences of that breach. Did the breach cause any harm, or was it merely collateral to the fraud?

This is an issue of causation and will depend on the specific duty owed by the seller and the particular circumstances in which the fraud was perpetrated. For example, consider the seller who wrongfully failed to keep confidential the details of its contract with the buyer, thus enabling the fraudster to discover the existence of the contract. Imagine that the fraudster then creates a confusingly similar email address to the seller's and persuades the buyer to make payment to the fraudster. It is unlikely that this breach can be said to have 'caused' the fraud, and thus the loss to the buyer. Put another way, the intervening act of the buyer in failing to identify the similar, but fraudulent, email breaks the chain of causation.

It may be that the minimum requirement is that the seller's actionable fault, enabling the fraudster to identify the opportunity, must also have enabled the means by which the fraud was perpetrated. For example, consider the seller who wrongfully failed to maintain adequate cyber security, thus enabling the fraudster to access the seller's email server and both (a) identify opportunity, and (b) send fraudulent payment instructions to the buyer. In this case, there is a more direct connection between the breach and the loss caused by the fraud.

In connection with arguments on causation, it is also necessary to consider remoteness. In the context that is here being discussed, the question of what would be reasonably foreseeable as the consequence of the seller's breach of duty is necessarily tied up with the question of what the content of that duty is. It is not an issue which can sensibly be addressed in the abstract, and parties would be well-advised to give careful consideration to the foreseeable consequences of a breach of duty when formulating what the appropriate duty is in any given case.

If these requirements can be met, then it is possible that the fault of the seller will give the buyer a defence by way of counterclaim. Consider a buyer who is sued for the contract price by the seller, having already paid the same to the fraudster. If the buyer can prove that an actionable breach by the seller caused the buyer to pay the fraudster, the buyer can counterclaim for damages to compensate the buyer for such loss. The sum lost is, naturally, the sum paid by the fraudster. This, by definition, is the same sum as the contract price and can thus set off entirely the seller's claim for the price. Insofar as the sum claimed by the seller is greater than the sum paid to the fraudster (such as due to the accrual of interest), this additional liability only accrued due to the seller's breach. The seller's claim for the same accordingly fails for circuity of action.

That was the situation where the seller was at fault in a situation where the buyer would otherwise be liable to pay again. The mirror situation is where the buyer is not liable to pay again (for example, because the fraudster contacts the seller's sole agent) but the buyer is then at fault for the fraudster identifying the opportunity. The difficulty in this instance in one of causation. As discussed above, it is unlikely that a breach of duty which merely enables the fraudster to identify an opportunity to perpetrate is legally causative of the subsequent loss resulting from the fraud. Unless the buyer's breach of duty in some way enabled the fraud, it is unlikely that the seller can claim against the buyer in such a case as this.

Agent as the source of the data

Rather than the counterparty (or the counterparty's own agent, whose actions can be attributed to the counterparty) being responsible for the fraudster identifying the opportunity and perpetrating the fraud, it may be that the victim's agent was the fraudster's data source.

If so, it is likely that the analysis will be similar to that where the counterparty is the source of the data. Whether the agent can be held liable will be a matter of identifying an actionable breach (in contract or, possibly, tort) and establishing that this breach caused the principal to suffer the loss of the fraud.

For example, consider a buyer who remains liable to pay the seller the contract price, despite having already paid the same to the fraudster, and who seeks to blame its agent. The section above explains the process that the buyer needs to go through, reading references in the previous section to 'the seller' as references to 'the buyer's agent', together with such logical changes as are required. In short, unless the fraudster not only identified the opportunity but also perpetrated the fraud as a result of the agent's breach, it is unlikely that the buyer will have a cause of action against the agent.

Service provider as the source of the data

It is possible that the fraudster identified the opportunity by means of information obtained from a person who was not directly interested in the underlying transactions. For example, the fraudster might have compromised a service provider to the victim of the fraud – such as an email provider, or the provider of a remote working or document sharing platform. Can the victim seek to recover from such third parties in respect of the fraud?

Again, as with the potential claim against a counterparty, the difficulty is in identifying a relevant duty owed by the service provider to the victim. If there is a direct contractual relationship, the question is whether there has been a breach of any of the terms of that contract. This may include the term implied by s.13 Supply of Goods and

Services Act 1982 that the service provider is to exercise 'reasonable skill and care' in the provision of those services, which could be argued to include ensuring that appropriate cyber security measures are employed to protect the integrity of a digital service platform.

In the absence of a contractual relationship, it is unlikely that the victim will have an action against the service provider in tort. Absent a contractual relationship, it is unlikely that the service provider will owe any relevant duties to the victim. For example, if a seller uses a particular document storage platform, there is no obvious reason why that platform owes duties to the seller's customers to maintain adequate cyber security. This may be different where the seller and buyer collaborate on a shared working platform, but in that case there is likely to be a direct contractual relationship between the provider and any user of its services (such as the seller and buyer, in this example).

Even if a service provider does fail to meet its duties to the victim, such as to maintain adequate cyber security, this does not necessarily mean that the service provider is responsible for any subsequent cyber fraud perpetrated on the victim. For the same reasons as in instances where the counter party is the source of the fraudster's information, it is likely that a service provider will not be liable where the breach has merely enabled the fraudster to identify an opportunity to perpetrate the fraud. Liability will likely only follow if the service provider's breach enabled the fraud in a more direct fashion. Even then, a claimant may encounter significant difficulties in establishing that its losses are not too remote as to be irrecoverable.

Independent wrongdoer as the source of the data

It is possible that the wrongdoer has acquired data from a third party which has committed an actionable wrong. Personal data such as usernames and passwords are, regrettably, sold. It may be possible to make the person who initially acquires such data, and (if different) the person who sells or transfers that data, liable for a cyber fraud perpetrated by using that data.

Consider a wrongdoer who illicitly obtains the login details for an online banking account. That wrongdoer sells this data to a third party, who uses it to perpetrate a fraud against the person whose account it is, making a payment from the victim's account to one held for the benefit of the fraudster. The victim of this fraud can pursue the fraudster directly. However, a free-standing cause of action also exists against the wrongdoer who obtained and sold the login details.

The basis of such a claim would be breach of confidence, a tort which imposes a duty to keep information confidential where the person with that information has notice that it is confidential. Where a person acquires data by dishonest means, or ought to realise that the information was acquired by dishonest means, there is little difficulty in establishing the necessary confidentiality. Distributing the data would then plainly be a breach of the obligation to keep the data confidential.

The situation where a person is entitled to access the information but does so for improper purposes and therefore acts wrongfully is no different. In *Aviva Insurance Ltd v Oliver* [2019] EWHC 2824 (Comm), an employee of the claimant insurer sold data about the insurer's customers to the defendant, who was then held liable for breach of confidentiality (as well as the tort of inducing a breach of contract and unlawful means conspiracy).

As to the remedies available, injunctions are available to pre-empt any breach of confidentiality. However, in cases of cyber fraud, the victim is more likely to be seeking damages. In this regard, the victim can claim damages to put them in the position as if the wrongdoer had not wrongfully obtained and distributed the data.

However, the chief difficulty in advancing this claim for damages will be remoteness of loss. The claimant will need to prove that the loss suffered was reasonably foreseeable to the wrongdoer who misappropriates the relevant personal data. Where that data includes log-in details for online banking, it seems reasonable that a person who (for example) sells that data to a third party can reasonably foresee its use to misappropriate the data subject's funds.

It is more difficult where the data does not so obviously expose the data subject to financial loss – for example, where the stolen data is a social media password. There are 2 arguments for the claimant in this situation. First, a social media account, for example, can be used as the first step in a chain to reset other passwords and obtain access to other accounts. Second, it is common that passwords are reused, so a social media password might be the same as the data subject's online banking password. Both these points could be reasonably foreseeable. Although the matter is to be considered prospectively, as at the time that the wrongdoer misappropriates the data, regard may also be had as to how the wrong in fact caused loss to the victim. So if a social media password was reused, then that could be relied on to support the argument that such an event was reasonably foreseeable.

In some jurisdictions, exemplary damages are available for breach of confidentiality. The point has not been determined in England & Wales, though Lindsay J in *Douglas v Hello! Ltd (No.3)* [2003] EWHC 786 (Ch) was prepared to assume, without deciding, that such damages were available.

CHAPTER FOUR

EXTORTION

Alongside payment frauds, extortion is probably the most well-known form of cyber crime. In broad terms, the wrongdoer contacts the victim directly and openly demands that the victim transfer an asset to the wrongdoer. The inducement for the victim to pay is a prior or threatened act of the wrongdoer, which the wrongdoer hopes will be a sufficient incentive to persuade the victim to make the transfer despite knowing that the transfer is without any legitimate basis.

The terminology of 'wrongdoer' is used here, rather than 'fraudster', because the act of extortion is not strictly speaking one of fraud; the extortion does not necessarily involve deception. Nevertheless, the similarity between the civil litigation of cyber fraud and the civil litigation of cyber extortion warrants discussion of the latter in this guide. Further, although the act of extortion itself may not involve a fraud, it is common that the necessary acts taken by the wrongdoer as a prelude to the extortion demand involved cyber fraud.

This guide considers blackmail cases as the archetypal extortion case. However, there is a distinction between blackmail and ransomware cases, the latter being the other common form of cyber extortion. Ransomware is not separately considered, given that what is said in respect of blackmail is largely directly applicable to ransomware cases.

In ransomware cases, the wrongdoer causes a form of malware (intentionally destructive software) on the victim's computer systems which causes the data on that system to be encrypted. The encryption prevents the victim from obtaining access to their own data without first inputting the decryption key. Once the victim has been excluded from accessing their own data, the wrongdoer will offer the victim the decryption key in exchange for payment.

In blackmail cases, the wrongdoer simply threatens to publish certain data which the wrongdoer believes that the victim is sufficiently keen to keep private that the victim would prefer to pay the extortion demand rather than risk publication: *cf.* definition in s.21(1) Theft Act 1968. By contrast with ransomware cases, a truly cyber-dependent form of wrongdoing, blackmail is simply a cyber-enabled form of wrongdoing. At its essence, there is nothing inherently different about cyber blackmail to 'analogue' blackmail; it is mentioned here for completeness given the increased prevalence of blackmail instances now that so much (potentially compromising) information can be obtained through digital means. Moreover, ransomware instances may carry an additional blackmail threat (to publish part of the encrypted data unless payment is made).

In rough terms, these forms of extortion may be respectively characterised as representing the 'carrot and stick' approach. In ransomware cases, the payment is made by the victim to obtain the 'carrot' of regaining access to their data; in blackmail cases, the payment is made to avoid the 'stick' of the relevant data being disclosed. However, this is not a perfect division. For example, a victim may feel compelled to pay the wrongdoer in a ransomware case for the primary purpose of avoiding the 'stick' of the breach in that victim's cyber security becoming public knowledge.

Blackmail

This section will be dealt with briefly given that blackmail has been an issue with which the law has been concerned for centuries. The manner in which blackmail is addressed in the modern law is relatively well-understood.

There have been a number of recent examples where threats are often made to disclose commercially sensitive data unless payment is made: e.g. *PML v Person(s) Unknown* [2018] EWHC 838 (QB) and *Clarkson Plc v Person or Persons Unknown* [2018] EWHC 417 (QB). As exemplified in those cases, the court is willing to grant *American*

Cynamid injunctions against persons unknown who have been involved in gaining unauthorised access to claimant parties' computer systems.

In such cases, the respondents are routinely ordered (by way of final relief) not to disclose the data, and may additionally or alternatively be asked to destroy any copies of the data that they have made: *cf. Bloomsbury Publishing v News Group Newspapers* [2003] 1 WLR 1633. As to the precise form of relief which may be sought, regard may be had to the Model Order in the Master of the Roll's Practice Guidance: Interim Non-Disclosure Orders. The form of non-disclosure order (NDO) is to be contrasted with interim NDOs which are intended to prevent the subject sharing information with (potentially) co-conspirators. Interim NDOs are discussed later in this guide.

The basis for this relief is that, ordinarily, the wrongdoer obtained the relevant data in circumstances which gave rise to an obligation on the wrongdoer to keep that data confidential: *Tchenguiz v Imerman* [2011] Fam 116 (CA) at [69] (Lord Neuberger MR). In the cyber context, the wrongdoer frequently obtains the data by obtaining illicit access to the victim's computer systems. This is itself sufficient to engage the obligation of confidentiality.

Similarly, the injunction may be sought on the basis that there is a misuse of private information. To found a claim in tort, a claimant must establish an objective, reasonable expectation of privacy in respect of the information at issue. If the claimant can do so, the court must balance that expectation against the wrongdoer's freedom of expression: *LJY v Persons Unknown* [2018] EMLR 19 at [25]-[26] (Warby J). The fact that blackmail is a misuse of freedom of expression "*will considerably reduce*" the weight given to that right: *LJY* at [29]-[30].

An additional ground on which an NDO may be secured is the tort of harassment, provided for by ss. 1 & 3 Protection from Harassment Act 1997. s.3(1) expressly contemplates that a civil claim may be brought in respect of an apprehended act of harassment. Where the threat made by the wrongdoer is to publish the data of the victim in multiple places or multiple times (which includes re-publishing if the victim succeeds in, for example, taking down the website where the material is first published), the tort can therefore be established: *LJY* at [33]-[37].

The fact that the data which is threatened to be published may be genuine does not excuse the wrongful nature of the harassment; it is only if the publication (including the circumstances in which it is made) is "*reasonable*" that a defence may be established: s.1(3) Protection from Harassment Act 1997; *LJY* at [40]. Publication to the world at large, against the demand of payment, is unlikely to be characterised as 'reasonable'. On the other hand, publication of the existence of the breach or of failures or wrongdoing by the victim to the appropriate authorities may be 'reasonable'. The more difficult issue may be whether demanding payment for the wrongdoer to refrain from notifying the appropriate authorities would be 'reasonable'. Critically, s.1(3) is concerned with the "*course of conduct*", being the threat to disclose, not exclusively the disclosure itself. It may be, therefore, that the extortive demand for payment is itself sufficient to make an otherwise reasonable course of conduct unreasonable.

A collateral remedy that is often sought by claimants is to ensure that public access is blocked to any websites which the confidential data is hosted on: *PML* at [7]. This may take the form of mandatory injunctions against the (likely innocent) hosting company, requiring them to prevent such access. Equally, the NDO against the defendant will commonly include a penal notice which explains that third parties who have notice of the order will be in contempt should they knowingly permit a breach of the order by the defendant. It may be that this is sufficient to persuade innocent hosts to take down the websites created in breach of the order, without the need for specific relief to be granted against the hosting company itself.

CHAPTER FIVE

OTHER WRONGFUL ACQUISITIONS

In July 2019, an Internet Service Provider reported that cyber attacks against UK business had tripled compared with the previous year. The report stated that many of the attached appeared to originate in China and, so far as could be established from successful attacks, seemed to be targeting intellectual and other digital property of the company.

Cyber fraud can also be used to appropriate assets other than purely digital assets. In the context of fraudulent payments, this guide has already considered the intervention of a fraudster diverting payment made under a genuine sale contract. Broadly the same principles apply where, rather than diverting the buyer's payment, the fraudster diverts the seller's goods. For example, if the fraudster uses a confusingly similar email address to that of the buyer's and persuades the seller to deliver the goods to the fraudster, the seller will probably be liable to the buyer for the non-delivery of the goods. This is for the reason, explained above, that the seller has failed to perform in accordance with the contract. It is no defence that the seller thought that it was acting in line with the buyer's instructions. Similarly, for the reasons above, if the fraudster duped the buyer's agent, who communicated the incorrect change in delivery details to the seller, then the buyer is likely to be liable.

Digital assets

So far as the wrongful acquisition of intellectual property and other commercially sensitive digital material is concerned, the victim of the wrongful acquisition will invariably want to restrict the use of distribution of that material. The relevant approach to this is largely the same as in cases of corporate blackmail, where publication of similar material is threatened in order to coerce the victim into meeting the wrongdoer's demand for payment. Most obviously, obligations of confidentiality will attach to the wrongfully-acquired information, which obligations will then form the basis for non-disclosure orders.

CHAPTER SIX

CRYPTO-ASSETS

Crypto-assets are a natural topic that follows in a discussion of cyber fraud, both because much cyber fraud concerns the appropriation of crypto-assets and because even where conventional assets are misappropriated they are frequently converted into crypto-assets.

The perceived anonymity and fungibility of crypto-assets, together with its volatile (and at times very significant) value, have made them appealing targets to cyber fraudsters. Given their purely-digital nature, they may also be readily misappropriated remotely. It is very difficult to compare year-on-year statistics, due to asset volatility and differences in in methodology, but what is clear is that each year for several years, misappropriation of crypto-assets through theft and fraud has been measured in billions of US Dollars.

Since the first edition of this guide, crypto-assets have proliferated in form and uptake. They have also become more integrated with conventional asset managers. Some nation states count certain crypto-assets as legal tender (e.g. Bitcoin in El Salvador), and other states have either posited (e.g. in England) or piloted (e.g. in in Hong Kong) a central bank-issued virtual currency on a blockchain. Meanwhile, other countries (e.g. China) have declared that crypto-transactions are illegal.

A cyber fraud litigator must therefore be prepared to engage with the issues that crypto-assets give rise to. In this chapter, some of the relevant factual and legal issues pertaining to crypto-assets are discussed. However, this is subject to at least two caveats:

First, it has previously been suggested that there is no more a law of (property in) cyberspace than there is a law of the horse: Easterbrook, F.H. 'Cyberspace and the Law of the Horse' (1996) University of Chicago Legal Forum 207. The same might be said of crypto-assets. At least at present, the law of crypto-assets is no different to the law applicable to other digital assets that have been the subject of litigation over time. Thus, existing principles can and should be applied to crypto-assets. Although crypto-assets will pose new challenges to the application of those principles, it does not mean that a new set of principles must be ascertained afresh.

Second, not all crypto-assets are minted equally. The nature of the different crypto-assets, including their technical features and the peculiarities of the blockchains on which they are recorded, may justify differentiation. Where the law has been found to apply in a certain way in respect of Bitcoin, it does not necessarily follow that the same applies to all crypto-currencies, let alone all crypto-assets or other data recorded on a blockchain.

As a straightforward example of this second point, the recent volatility of Bitcoin is such that the court has previously refused to accept it as adequate security for costs: *Tulip Trading v Bitcoin Association BSV* [2022] EWHC 2 (Ch) (though to opposite effect, see *Hague v Cordiner (No. 2)* [2020] NSWDC 23). That is, however, a generalisation and it is possible that some crypto-assets, such as mainstream stablecoins, would be more acceptable: Bell, C. & Whitehouse, C. 'Stablecoins as security? Never say tether' (2022) 4 JIBFL 266.

Additional caveats/limitations are identified in a subsequent section.

What are crypto-assets?

At essence, a crypto-asset is a notional or actual asset represented by a virtual token, transactions in respect of which are recorded on a cryptographically-secured blockchain.

Crypto-assets have both a public and a private key. The public key may be thought of as the address of the asset, similar in some respects to an account number in conventional banking. The private key is a passcode, required before any transaction can be made using the crypto-asset. The public and private keys can be stored on any medium – such as written down on paper, or stored as a digital file on a computer. However, they are frequently lodged with third party service providers, such as crypto-asset exchanges, who store the public and private keys of multiple crypto-assets for any one person and provide a platform on which an owner of crypto-assets can track and transact with their assets. Alternatively, public and private keys can be stored in virtual wallets, which can either be 'hot' (permanently connected to internet) or 'cold' and commonly take the form of phone apps or physical hardware such as USB devices.

A person with knowledge of both the public and the private key has the power to transact with the crypto-asset. When each transaction takes place, it is verified by reference to the blockchain and a permanent record of the transaction (identifying the asset, the sending public address and the receiving public address) is recorded on the blockchain. The blockchain at essence is simply an immutable ledger of transactions. It records every transaction that has taken place in respect of a given token, which is the underlying digital asset.

There is also a distinction to be drawn between permissionless blockchains and permissioned (i.e. private) blockchains. In the case of permissionless blockchains, the blockchain is publicly available for scrutiny. The blockchain is truly decentralised; the record of all entries on the blockchain is stored on multiple nodes, and anyone can have access to and view the blockchain. However, this is not necessarily the case in permissioned blockchains, where a regulating party controls who may access the transaction history of the blockchain. The regulating party in a permissioned blockchain will be responsible for nominating the nodes on which the blockchain is stored, and may ensure that all of the nodes are within the control of the regulating party (or at least not publicly available).

Where the transaction history can be publicly viewed, in permissionless or some permissioned blockchains, it is possible to identify the public key (approximately equivalent to the account) which into which the fraudulent proceeds may be traced. The nature of the open, distributed ledger system means that each transaction involving (for example)

Bitcoin is a matter of public record. What is more difficult is establishing the identity of the person who has access to any particular crypto-asset at any given time – i.e. who holds the private key necessary to access the relevant crypto-asset.

The term crypto-asset is used in this guide, rather than crypto-currency, because crypto-assets are not limited to crypto-currencies such as Bitcoin.

Non-Fungible Tokens, or NFTs, are a popular example. At their most basic, NFTs are limited collections of tokens, whose sole value is in their scarcity. As such the value is whatever subjective worth is attributed to control over a given token. Making an analogue comparison, an artist may create 100 limited edition prints. The artist can sell them at whatever price the artist likes, but the value of a given print is in it being part of a limited collection and is determined by the subjective factor of what others would be prepared to pay for it. However, the basic NFT is merely a digital token, not an artwork. NFTs have commonly been associated with particular images, but do not typically carry control over the use of that image. They are better thought of as certificates of authenticity.

That said, NFTs can come with a package of associated rights which are not limited to mere control over the digital token. This can be seen in two examples.

First, the widely known 'Bored Ape' NFT collection has an associated cryptocurrency called 'ApeCoin'. Control over a given 'BoredApe' NFT gives the controller the ability to claim ApeCoin at certain times.

Second, the artist Damien Hirst released a series of unique physical artworks, each of which was also associated with an individual NFTs. Purchasers of a given artwork would receive both the physical painting and control over the relevant NFT. However, after a year, the person then with control was required either to relinquish the physical painting to Damien Hirst for destruction or to allow the NFT to be 'burned' (i.e. cancelled and destroyed).

These examples demonstrate that there are two features of crypto-assets that litigators should be aware of. First, considering the example of an asset trace into a particular crypto-asset, it is not enough merely to be concerned with custody of the relevant token (e.g. by obtaining a proprietary injunction in respect of a Bored Ape NFT); regard must also to be had as to whether there are collateral benefits to the fraudster's 'possession' of the asset (e.g. the opportunity to benefit from airdrops of ApeCoin) that need to be considered. Second, digital tokens are not necessarily persistent; depending on the blockchain and the asset, the token can be burned by a third party and thus permanently lost.

Crypto-currencies and NFTs have been mentioned thus far. These are the most frequently encountered crypto-assets in fraud litigation. However, litigators should be alive to the very wide variety of tokens types that come within the umbrella term 'crypto-assets'.

Limitations to current judicial consideration of crypto-assets

There have been numerous occasions on which the courts have been required to consider legal issues in respect of crypto-assets. In broad terms, courts have taken a consistent approach to crypto-assets, both as between different courts in the jurisdiction of England & Wales, and as between those courts and courts in other jurisdictions. However, the judgments that have become public on these issues are very often not conclusive on the underlying legal issues for one or more of the following reasons:

First, the judgments are determinations of interim applications, such that there is no need to make a final determination on the relevant legal issues. For example, in *Vorotyntseva v Money-4 Ltd (T/A Nebus.com)* [2018] EWHC 2596 (Ch), the court only held that there was a good arguable case that Bitcoin and Etherium were choses in possession.

Second, the hearings are attended by one party only, such that the court does not have the benefit of adversarial argument on important points of principle. For example, in *Jones v Persons Unknown* [2022] EWHC 2543 (Comm), there was no party other than the applicant in attendance and so no party to argue against the proposition that Bitcoin constituted a chose in possession. It is for this reason that such cases may not be cited as authorities: Practice Direction (Citation of Authorities) [2001] 1 WLR 1001.

Third, where hearings are attended by parties other than the claimant or applicant, the relevant legal issues are either common ground or not otherwise disputed. For example, in *Wang v Derby* [2021] EWHC 3054 (Comm), it was common ground between the parties that Tezos were an item of property, the issue being whether that property was held on trust. In *LMN v Bitfly* [2022] EWHC 2954 (Comm), the various exchanges that were defendants to the claim for disclosure orders did not dispute the argument that six different crypto-currencies all constituted items of personal property.

One reason why the relevant legal issues were not argued may be that the relevant parties did not consider there to be any legal merit in doing so. However, as briefly addressed below, there is often sufficient uncertainty on the legal position to justify the argument. The more likely reason seems to be that it is not in the interests of the parties to dispute these issues. However, this has prevented the issues being fully considered on an adversarial stage. There is scope for an amicus curiae brief to address these points, but that is reliant on an appropriate case arising and a suitably motivated intervener becoming involved.

These matters need to be borne in mind when considering the existing law as applied to crypto-assets.

Are crypto-assets property?

The first question often asked is as to the nature of crypto-assets. Specifically, are they choses in possession, some form of chose in action, or something else entirely?

This issue has been answered, albeit non-authoritatively, by the Legal Statement on Cryptoassets and Smart Contracts, published on 18 November 2019 by the UK Jurisdiction Taskforce. There, it was concluded that a crypto-asset could be treated as property, as it met the criteria set out in *National Provincial Bank v Ainsworth* [1965] AC 1175, even though it did not meet a narrow definition of a chose in action and could not be a chose in possession as, being intangible, the asset could not be possessed.

The Legal Statement on the proprietary nature of crypto-assets was endorsed in *AA v Persons Unknown* [2020] 4 WLR 35 at [56]-[61] (Bryan J), frequently referred to (e.g. *LMN v Bitfly* [2022] EWHC 2954 (Comm) at [19] (Butcher J)). On the basis that certain crypto-currencies were realistically capable of being property, the judge granted proprietary injunctions against the person unknown who issued a ransom demand, the person unknown who holds specified Bitcoins, and the two entities which operated the crypto-asset exchange.

The approach in *AA*, provisionally treating crypto-currencies as property, matches the approach taken in *B2C2 v Quoine* [2019] SGHC(I) 03 at [142] (though, as noted on appeal, this was common ground between the parties; the appeal court expressly left open the question whether crypto-assets could be the subject of a trust: [2020] SGCA(I) 02 at [5]-[6]) and *Ruscoe & Moore v Cryptopia Limited* [2020] NZHC 728 (where it was held that crypto-assets were property held on trust in a liquidation).

A slightly different view was taken in *Fetch-ai Ltd v Persons Unknown* [2021] EWHC 2254 (Comm), which held that certain crypto-currencies were choses in action. However, the end result is materially the same – it is property and capable of protection as such. Ultimately, the courts have been content to find that crypto-assets should be susceptible to freezing orders, such that they should be property of some description: *cf. DPP v Briedis* [2021] EWHC 3155 (Admin). The courts have therefore been content to proceed on the proprietary basis, even if the issue as to which precise class of property these assets belong to is expressly left open: e.g. *Robertson v Persons Unknown* (unreported, 15 July 2019).

It is also worth noting that the criminal courts in England have made confiscation orders in respect of crypto-currencies, considering such assets to come within the definition of property in s.84(1) Proceeds of Crime Act 2002: *R v Teresko (Serejs)* [2018] Crim LR 81. However, the definition of property in s.84 is broader than property at common law, and in that respect is similar to s.436 Insolvency Act 1986: *cf. Bristol Airport Plc v Powdrill* [1990] Ch 744 (CA). In *DPP v Briedis* [2021] EWHC 3155 (Admin), the court granted a property freezing order under s.245A Proceeds of Crime Act 2002 in respect of various crypto-currencies, again on the basis of the broad definition of property in s.316(4)(c).

In *Osbourne v Persons Unknown* [2022] EWHC 1021, it was held that NFTs, like crypto-currencies, could be treated as property.

Similar views have been reached in other jurisdictions. For example, freezing injunctions have been made in Hong Kong in respect of crypto-currencies (*Yan Yu Ying v Leong Wing Hei* [2021] HKCFI 3160 and *Samara v Dan* [2019] HKCFI 2718), and in Singapore in respect of NFTs (*Janesh s/o Rajkumar v Unknown Person ("CHEFPIERRE")* [2022] SGHC 264).

These civil decisions have all been limited to finding a good arguable case. Recently, *Jones v Persons Unknown* [2022] EWHC 2543 (Comm) in England and *Samara v Dan* [2022] HKCFI 1254 in Hong Kong have granted final relief based on the proprietary status. However, in each case it was without attendance from the defendants. (In *Samara*, it appears that the defendant did raise arguments in defence – not including that Bitcoin were not legal property – but did not attend and was not represented at the hearing.)

The proprietary status of crypto-assets is thus the currently-prevailing view, at least in part because it is convenient to litigants and attractive to the courts that the full range of proprietary remedies be available in respect of misappropriated crypto-assets. However, arguments have been raised to the contrary (beyond the doubts expressed in judgments as to how crypto-assets can fit the apparent requirements of choses in possession or choses in action). For example, it may fairly be said that the digital assets do not, as such, exist. All that exists is a record of data entries (recording notional transfers of a notional asset), with the holder of a particular private key having at any one time the power to make the next entry in the ledger: Fox, D. 'Digital assets as transactional power' (2022) 1 JIBFL 3.

The Law Commission has recently published a consultation paper, proposing that the proprietary status of crypto-assets should be recognised on an entirely new basis, proposing a new category of property alongside and distinct from the existing property regime at common law.

It remains to be seen whether the consultation paper is supported by the industry, and then whether the Law Commission is invited to prepare draft legislation, and then whether that gets passed into English law. However, it is clear that the discussion on the proprietary status (or not) of crypto-assets (or of some crypto-assets but not others) is not yet concluded.

Consequence of any proprietary status

Whether crypto-assets are property is particularly relevant in cases of cyber fraud because the nature of the crypto-asset determines the forms of interim and final relief which may be available in respect of any impugned transaction. For example, can a party obtain a proprietary injunction in respect of crypto-assets? Can they be subject to a trust? Can they be followed, or can value be traced through them? So far, it seems that the answer to these questions is 'yes', but for the reasons explained above that answer has not yet been conclusively determined.

The specific nature of the crypto-assets might also here give reason to distinguish between different classes of asset. Assuming that all crypto-assets are capable of being property, if a litigant sought to recover a BoredApe NFT they would be looking to regain control over the specific NFT that had been misappropriated. That would naturally follow from the fact that each such NFT is unique from every other NFT, so although a litigant might be satisfied by financial compensation for their loss, the law would recognise their right to the return of that which was taken – just as with a unique physical artwork.

Does the same apply to Bitcoin? As a crypto-currency, its utility is its fungibility and transferability as a mode of payment. Generally, individuals do not regard as relevant the specific Bitcoin that they hold, just the overall quantity of Bitcoin. An analogy may be drawn with bank notes, which are capable of individual identification by serial code but which are generally treated as being entirely fungible with an equivalent note. However, as with bank notes, it is conceivable that some Bitcoin will be unusually valuable. For example, the first Bitcoin ever mined may have additional value in the same way that a bank note with serial code 00001 might be worth more than its face value. Might it be that Bitcoin are treated differently to BoredApe NFTs, or even that some Bitcoin are treated differently to other Bitcoin?

These issues also raise an entirely unresolved legal question of whether, and if so how, the nemo dat principle applies to crypto-assets. The general rule is that a person can generally only transfer the interest that they have. Consider a crypto-asset which is stolen (e.g. by the fraudster obtaining illicit access to the victim's hot wallet). If that crypto-asset is personal property, the victim of the theft retains possessory title to the asset and any transferee of the asset, even if they were a bona fide purchaser of the asset, receives no more than the thief's inferior possessory title. It would therefore be open to a person who had their Bitcoin stolen to seek recovery of the specific Bitcoin as against the current holder, even if the current holder could not otherwise be held liable. Although that might be understandable in the case of unique crypto-assets such as NFTs, the result is more difficult to justify in the case of crypto-assets which tend to be used merely as a means of payment.

Considerations in respect of interim protection

As is evident from the cases on crypto-assets to date, litigants are often legitimately concerned to protect their position by seeking freezing or proprietary injunctions in respect of crypto-assets. The unusual nature of crypto-assets gives rise to a number of additional considerations, beyond those which any application for such injunctions should have regard to.

First, where the claim concerns the recovery of damages or other value, claimants should consider the risks inherent in freezing crypto-assets. Given the significant volatility in the value of such assets, regard should be had to the risk of injuncting the defendant from transacting with such assets, only to be liable to compensate the defendant if the injunction is subsequently found not to be justified.

Consider a case where the claim fails, and the defendant seeks compensation under the standard cross-undertaking in damages. The defendant alleges that they would have sold their crypto-assets shortly before a significant drop in the value of such assets. The claimant's freezing injunction prevented the sale taking place, such that the defendant must now compensate the defendant for the difference between the current value of the asset and the value at their height of the market.

A claimant will wish to weigh the risk of this happening against the benefit to be had by freezing a potentially valuable asset. There have been instances of claimants seeking freezing injunctions which specifically exclude any crypto-assets held by the defendant due to this concern. However, litigants should be conscious that the court will scrutinise any suggestion by the defendant that, but for the freezing injunction, they would have entered into particularly profitable trades: e.g. *Ennismore Fund Management v Fenris Consulting Ltd* [2022] UKPC 27.

Toma v Murray [2020] EWHC 2295 (Ch) is a case which indicates that the issue of volatility may affect the court's discretion, even where the claimant is prepared to take on the risk in respect of volatility. In *Toma*, the court indicated that the volatility of Bitcoin was a factor militating against granting a freezing injunction. *Toma* also suggests a possible mitigation to the risk of a defendant being unable to act when the market falls, in that the judge considered a proposal for a regime enabling the sale of a frozen asset where it took place with the claimant's consent.

Second, as a continuation of the previous point, claimants should be prepared to provide fortification of their cross-undertaking in damages. The court may take the view that the fortification should be significant to cover off the possibility of a significant loss resulting from market volatility.

Third, litigants would be well-advised to consider both how to preserve the crypto-asset itself and how to preserve any rights that may be associated with the asset. The possibility of, for example, an NFT carrying associated rights has been discussed above. Where those rights are valuable, the claimant will wish to preserve that value, rather than permit the defendant to continue to enjoy the fruits of the frozen crypto-asset.

The risk of destruction should also be born in mind. Taking the example of the Damien Hirst NFTs referred to earlier, it would be self-defeating for a claimant to freeze the relevant NFT, only for the defendant then to elect to retain the physical artwork and for Damien Hirst to burn the NFT. Perhaps Damien Hirst could be given notice of the freezing injunction in this hypothetical, and the claimant would then need to give thought to the practical ramifications of this.

Fourth, following on from guarding against the risk of a crypto-asset being burned, the claimant may wish to use the burn process as a means by which to preserve value.

The central authority of some crypto-assets, including some crypto-currencies, retains the power to burn crypto-assets. A conventional approach to the interim preservation of such assets would be to seek a freezing injunction against the holder of the crypto-asset, injuncting them against dealing with the asset. The claimant may be concerned about the likelihood of a defendant – such as a cyber fraudster – complying with such an order. Instead, the claimant may hope that the crypto-assets are within the control of a third party, such as an exchange, who can be given notice of the injunction and will exclude the defendant's access to the same (perhaps even by moving the impugned assets into a segregated account held with the exchange). That may be successful, or it may not.

An alternative approach could be to obtain final relief against the central authority of the crypto-asset, such as the issuer of the crypto-currency. The claimant could apply for an order which required the issuer to burn the crypto-asset which was in the hands of the fraudster, and to mint a replacement crypto-asset which would then be transferred to the claimant (or, perhaps more likely, an interim receiver). The interim receiver could be used in the conventional approach discussed above, so long as there was a third party controller who would comply. The benefit of this alternative approach is that it does not rely on any holder/controller of the asset being compliant, only the issuer of the asset. The difficulty is that this approach requires a central controller, which is not the case for crypto-assets such as Bitcoin.

Tracing crypto-asset transactions

Say the victim of a cyber fraud has been induced to transfer crypto-assets to a third party, or alternatively has traced conventional proceeds of fraud (such as money in a bank account) into a crypto-asset. How does the potential claimant go about seeking disclosure as to what happened with that crypto-asset, where the traceable proceeds of any fraud may now be located, and the identity of those persons holding the assets?

There are third party service providers who will conduct an analysis of publicly available information to track transfers of crypto-assets. As an example of this, see *AA v Persons Unknown* [2020] 4 WLR 35 at [13].

This form of public tracking is possible with certain forms of crypto-assets, such as Bitcoin (in *AA*), because those crypto-assets are stored on permissionless or unpermissioned (i.e. public) blockchains.

Once a public key is identified which appears to be associated with the crypto-asset being tracked, the claimant will need to identify the person who has control over that public key. To obtain this information, the most obvious target (as in *Robertson*) is a crypto-asset exchange which is associated with that public key. Again, third party service providers are able in some cases to identify from the public record the exchange which is likely to be associated with a given public key.

Exchanges may have KYC obligations and thus may hold sufficient information to enable to identity of particular holders of crypto-assets to be discovered. Other targets for disclosure orders may present themselves, such as parties receiving transfers from (or making transfers to) the crypto-asset holder.

As to how the information is obtained from the exchange, a similar approach is taken to obtaining equivalent information from a bank about that bank's customer. In *Robertson*, for example, the information was sought by means of a *Bankers Trust* order against the UK branch of a USA-headquartered company.

It is possible to question whether the extension of the *Bankers Trust* jurisdiction to crypto-asset exchanges is a valid one. Generally, *Bankers Trust* is employed against banks and other financial institutions. However, there is no requirement that the target of *Bankers Trust* disclosure be a bank: e.g. *Hickox v Dickinson* [2020] EWHC 2520 (Ch). Moreover, it may be said that an exchange is holding assets for a given individual in the same way that a bank holds assets for a given individual. Both may be subject to a provider-customer relationship governed by a contract, which may include confidentiality terms. The conclusion that *Bankers Trust* orders are available against exchanges is supported by the decision in *AA* that crypto-assets are property, together with the numerous instances since where *Bankers Trust* orders have been made (though none where the exchanges have disputed the applicability of the relevant jurisdiction).

In the event that a *Bankers Trust* order is not available, it would be possible to seek information under the *Norwich Pharmacal* jurisdiction or under CPR 25.1(1)(g).

This analysis has so far proceeded on the basis that one is tracing through crypto-asset transactions which are a matter of public record, such as in a permissionless system. If the transaction history is not publicly available, there is the necessary prior step of obtaining access to the history before one can trace the crypto-asset transactions and then seek to identify who is holding any traceable proceeds. In such cases, disclosure of the transaction history will need to be sought from a person who has access to the relevant information. This will normally be the regulator of the permissioned blockchain, but may equally be any person who has access to that history for whatever reason (such as because they have been nominated as a node by the regulator).

Difficulties with exchanges

LMN v Bitflyer [2022] EWHC 2954 (Comm) illustrates, and provides a solution, for a common problem encountered with crypto-related businesses. The precise corporate structure operating the relevant business (for example, an exchange) is often unclear. It may be possible to identify various corporate entities which have been formed in various different jurisdictions. However, the business – including its terms – may be unclear on precisely which entity is performing which function.

There are two significant issues that are encountered in this regard. First, for any disclosure order to be useful, it needs to be against the person who has the relevant documents to disclose. If disclosure is sought against one entity within a business structure, but the documents are held by a different entity, it may be that the first entity cannot provide the relevant documentation. Second, even if the correct entity for disclosure is identified, the applicant may seek collateral non-disclosure orders to guard against tipping off. If so, the applicant would want the orders to be effective against the entire business with which the disclosure target is identified, not just the target entity and no other related entity.

A solution to both these issues was deployed in *LMN*. The solution was to name as defendants both the known or suspected corporate entity and a class of persons unknown by reference to the terms on which the relevant business operated. Thus Binance Holdings Limited was the second defendant in LMN and an additional defendant was "*PERSONS UNKNOWN (BINANCE) (being the individuals or companies or other entities who are identified in the Binance.com platform's terms and conditions as Binance Operators but not the Second Defendant)*"; see at [41]. Moreover, in respect of confidentiality, the initial order provided that "*if the Defendants contacted their subsidiaries about the claim, they should obtain an undertaking from those subsidiaries that they should not inform others about the claim, in a form which was annexed to the order*": [31] (though this was not continued: [46]). For Butcher J's explanation of these points, see [11].

Pre-empting misappropriation of crypto-assets

The nature of crypto-assets is that wrongful acts may be perpetrated in respect of the assets which do not directly involve misappropriation (at least in the immediate term) of the crypto-asset itself.

For example, as a preparatory step towards misappropriating a crypto-asset, a fraudster may acquire the private key which relates to a particular crypto-asset. The private key may be encrypted in some way, but it may be that the fraudsters are expected to be able to defeat this encryption given time. Naturally, the legitimate 'owner' of the crypto-asset in these circumstances will seek to prevent any misappropriation of the crypto-asset taking place, rather than simply wait for the misappropriation to occur and then go about pursuing the fraudster for the crypto-asset's return.

In effect, this is a situation where a misappropriation of personal data (the private key) has taken place which is expected to lead to the misappropriation of property (the crypto-asset). The private key itself is not property; as pure information, it cannot have proprietary status: *Your Response Limited v Datateam Business Media Limited* [2014] EWCA Civ 281. If the private key is stored and stolen on a physical medium, such as a USB device, then that physical medium may be the claimant's property and orders can be sought in respect of that property (distinct from the crypto-assets directly). However, the case is more difficult where the private key is simply misappropriated from a purely digital medium – for example, it may be copied from an encrypted digital folder which is stored with a cloud data provider.

It may be that the attempt to decrypt the private key constitutes a breach of confidence by the fraudsters, who must realise that the encrypted information is confidential. Alternatively, any use of the decrypted private key would certainly constitute a breach of confidentiality – and the use of that private key to fraudulently misappropriate the underlying crypto-asset would be a further wrong (such as the tort of conversion). The legitimate owner of the crypto-asset may apply for a *quia timet* injunction against the wrongdoers (with notice to, for example, any crypto-asset exchange which holds the crypto-assets to the legitimate owner's account) to prevent these wrongs from taking place.

Further or alternatively, as in *Robinson*, an asset preservation order could be sought over the crypto-assets in anticipation that there will in the near future (if the private key is decrypted) be the subject of a serious issue to be tried as to the proprietary interests in those crypto-assets.

Governing law of crypto-assets

The natural starting point, as identified by the Financial Markets Law Committee in their 2018 FinTech report, is that the parties' choice of law should prevail, if present. In a distributed ledger technology system, this choice will probably be the choice that all network participants subscribe to when seeking accession to the system. Further, insofar as the specific crypto-asset transaction was governed by a contract, that contract may provide additional (or conflicting) indications as to the direct parties' choice of law.

In the absence of any such express or implied choice, recourse may be had to the relevant conflicts rules insofar as the underlying transaction is concerned. Generally, the validity of a transfer of movable property (such as, *ex hypothesi*, a crypto-asset) is determined by the location of the asset (its lex situs). Location is a difficult issue to determine. The asset itself is only notional, being represented by a token whose only existence is in the record of its transfers. That record may be on a distributed ledger which is located on numerous different equally-authoritative nodes in disparate jurisdictions.

If the asset cannot be sensibly said to be 'located' in any given jurisdiction, it may be sensible to consider the law which governs the underlying transaction pursuant to which the crypto-asset was transferred. Thus, where a crypto-asset is sold pursuant to a contract, Art.4 of the Rome I Regulation identifies what the governing law of the contract is to be. It may be argued that the governing law of the contract can be said to be the governing law of the crypto-asset transfer, in the event that the normal rules as to property transfers cannot apply.

As to the applicable law when addressing how the tracing process is to operate, this is again somewhat unclear. Under English law, tracing is not a remedy but merely a process. As such, it may be seen as being a procedural mechanism and thus the law applicable to it is the law of the jurisdiction seised of the matter. If a claim is made in England concerning the tracing of crypto-assets, the English law of tracing will operate insofar as the crypto-assets may be said to be trust property. (The applicable law when addressing the existence of trusts is dealt with in the procedural guidance chapter of this guide.)

The issue of applicable law has not often been considered by the courts. In *Ion Science Ltd v Persons Unknown* (unreported, 21 December 2020)

(Commercial Court), Butcher J considered that English law applied to a fraudulent misappropriation of crypto-assets. This decision was made on two alternative bases:

First, the judge held that the relevant damage for any tortious claim occurred in England. This (interim) conclusion was itself based on either of two reasons. The Judge first relied on the fact that England was the jurisdiction of the bank account which funded the relevant crypto account. The judge also considered it relevant that the fraud was perpetrated when the victim gave remote access to his computer which was located in England.

Second, the judge held that the crypto-assets themselves were located in England. This was on the basis that it has been posited that the lex situs of crypto-assets is the jurisdiction in which the owner is domiciled. This conclusion fits with the approach of the UK Jurisdiction Taskforce, who considered that decentralised assets should be located in the place where there is central control, such that the location of the controller determines the location of the asset. It has also been supported in *Tulip Trading Ltd v Bitcoin Association for BSV* [2022] EWHC 667 (Ch) at [147]-[149] (Falk J) and in *LMN v Bitflyer* [2022] EWHC 2954 (Comm) at [20] (Butcher J), the judge in both cases indicating that the issue of domicile is not the exclusive relevant factor, with consistency between domicile and residence or place of business also being relevant.

Demonstrating a developing consistency, HMRC has declared domicile to be the relevant criterion when determining whether crypto-assets are susceptible to UK tax in its guidance, 'Cryptoassets: Tax for Individuals'.

The use of domicile as identifying the lex situs is not free from difficulty. For example, consider a crypto-asset which is co-owned by two people who are domiciled in different jurisdictions. Is the asset notionally located in one or both or neither jurisdiction? It may be that the analysis should be the identification of the most closely connected jurisdiction, with the domicile of an owner being the most obvious way to do so. However, it is an unsatisfactory result to say that in the case of joint owners one must identify which owner is most closely associated with the crypto-asset.

A further difficulty is that a crypto-asset may be capable of identification on the blockchain. It may also be capable of being identified as being associated with a particular exchange. However, for so long as the identity of the owner is unknown, the owner's domicile is unknown. The result is that a specific crypto-asset can be identified, and a person with current control over the asset identified, but the lex situs of that asset is necessarily unknown and unknowable until the owner is identified.

This leads to an alternative way to identify the lex situs: identifying the means by which the crypto-assets can be accessed and realised – i.e. the private key. If the holder of the crypto-asset has their private key written down on a piece of paper, the location of that paper may be said to represent the 'location' of the crypto-assets. Similarly, if the private key is stored on a computer, the location of the computer's hard-drive will be the relevant location. By logical extension, if the private key is stored on a cloud server only, then the crypto-assets would be located wherever the server bases are – unless, of course, the storage form used is decentralised cloud storage, in which case the relevant data could be spread across different nodes in disparate jurisdictions. Consider also the difficulties caused by the private key (which is merely a passcode) being duplicated and stored in different locations – such as where a person has a written record of the private key both at home and at work, which may be located in different jurisdictions.

Arguably, the position may be simpler where the private key is deposited with a crypto-asset exchange rather than being held personally. Where the holder of a crypto-asset has elected to deposit the private key with an exchange, it may be deemed that the holder has similarly deposited the crypto-asset. Thus, the location of the exchange will determine the location of the crypto-asset. The same might be said to apply to any hot wallet system.

This is an instance where having a rule is arguably more important than the rule being principled. However, the common law struggles with arriving at an unprincipled position, so such a move would need to be dictated by legislation.

Extent of duties owed by blockchain facilitators

In *Tulip Trading v Bitcoin Association BSV* [2022] EWHC 667 (Ch), the claimant sought to argue that a range of blockchain developers owed him various duties in tort and equity. He claimed to have been the victim of theft, where his assets had been stolen. The claimant argued that the developers of the blockchain itself could, in theory, write code into the blockchain to enable the allegedly wrongful transactions to be reversed. The claimant sought to rely on this ability to say that the developers therefore had a responsibility to him to take steps to facilitate the return of his stolen assets.

That claim was dismissed at a summary level, though the judgment is currently under appeal. Irrespective of the appeal's success, *Tulip Trading* indicates that litigants will explore the duties to be implied into relationships between crypto market participants. Rather than blockchain developers, the most likely focus of this interest will be on the exchanges.

The extent to which a crypto-asset exchange may be seen as equivalent to a bank remains to be seen. Although crypto-assets now seem to be recognised as property, that does not mean that they are necessarily to be seen as equivalent to money (and there are many strong arguments made that they should not be). In this regard, Butcher J explained that the (anonymised) exchange in *LMN v Bitflyer* [2022] EWHC 2954 (Comm) considered that "*it does not hold the cryptocurrencies on trust. Rather, it holds cryptocurrency in its own name and, in a manner analogous to conventional banking, owes a personal obligation to pay the relevant amount to each customer.*"

This is an important issue to consider, as it has ramifications on the ability of claimants to seek both interim and substantive relief against the exchanges. It may well also be that there is not a one-size-fits-all approach, with the duties owed by different exchanges varying depending on their contractual terms, the manner in which they hold (or do not hold) crypto-assets for their customers, and the extent of the services provided to customers.

In *AA*, it was alleged that the exchange held the Bitcoins as constructive trustee for the victim, alternatively that the exchange is amenable to a restitutionary claim because they are holding assets which belong to the victim and to which the exchange has no right. Bryan J was prepared to accept that there was at least a serious issue to be tried as to whether there was a proprietary claim to be made against the exchange, though suggested that it was less clear than the direct claim against the apparent wrongdoers: *AA* at [63]-[64].

In *AA*, this was used as a means to evade the difficulty of *AB Bank* and the perceived inability to seek disclosure orders against third parties located outside of the jurisdiction. By making direct claims against the exchange, and founding a proprietary injunction, the claimant there was permitted to bring the exchange within gateway (3) (necessary and proper party) and to seek disclosure orders which were ancillary to the primary proprietary injunction: *AA* at [70] & [81].

The point does not appear to have been discussed in *AA*, but in *Robertson* the question was raised as to why a direct cause of action was being pursued against the exchange, as well as the apparent wrongdoers. By comparison, it would be unusual to bring claims against a bank as well as a fraudster in a classic case of cyber fraud. The claimant in *Robertson* sought to rely on the fact that the exchange had the private key, necessary to transfer the Bitcoins, so direct relief was required as against the exchange to transfer the Bitcoins back to the claimant (as was the substantive relief sought).

However, it is unclear why the ability of the exchange to transfer the Bitcoins held in the exchange's client's account is any different from the ability of a bank to transfer money held in the bank's customer's account. Had the claimant in *Robertson* sought and obtained only an order against the Bitcoin holder of the return of the Bitcoins, the claimant would have been able to enforce that order in the ordinary way against the Bitcoins held with the exchange.

This is not a stale distinction. Consider the situation where the exchange was based in a foreign jurisdiction; it is conceivable that the foreign jurisdiction might enforce an English judgment debt against the exchange, but would refuse to allow an English judgment against the Bitcoin holder to be enforced against the Bitcoins held by the exchange. (It should be noted that *Robertson* did not proceed past the interim stage of proceedings; the identified recipient returned the Bitcoins without the court ordering him, or the exchange, to do so.)

The extent to which the manner in which an exchange operates may be seen as analogous to a bank may also have a bearing on the duties owed by the exchange. Earlier in this guide, there was a discussion of a bank's *Quincecare* duty – the implied duty to guard against fraudulent payments being made out of the customer's account. It is an open issue as to whether the duty could be extended beyond traditional banks. In *Hamblin v World First* [2020] EWHC 2383 (Comm), it was suggested that the duty might be owed by an e-money institution. It is possible that the duty could also be owed by an exchange.

CHAPTER SEVEN

PROCEDURAL GUIDANCE

The courts are willing to engage with the difficulties posed by cyber fraud litigation, and will adapt remedies and procedures as required to meet these new challenges. Sometimes this is as simple as applying well-established legal method to new factual situations, but it is also occasionally necessary in cyber fraud litigation to extend the current state of the law.

When making inroads into previously uncanvassed areas in cyber fraud litigation, litigants would be well-advised to be frank with the court. It also means being scrupulous in ensuring proper compliance with procedural requirements – including in respect of full and frank disclosure. There have been several high-profile recent cases (e.g. *Punjab National Bank v Srinivasan* [2019] UKHC 89 (Ch)) where freezing injunctions and other orders have been set aside for material non-disclosure. This can result in otherwise-valid relief being refused, adverse costs orders being made and in extreme cases the entire litigation being derailed. For example, in fraudulent payment cases, the discharge of a freezing injunction for non-disclosure could be the difference between being able to make an effective recovery against the fraudster and being deprived of that opportunity.

Moreover, litigators would be well-advised to err on the side of caution – and thus 'over-' disclosure. In *Wang v Real Assets Global Opportunity Fund I Limited* (19 August 2022, unreported), the BVI Commercial Court discharged an interim order appointing provisional liquidators. The applicant had applied without notice for the appointment of interim receivers over shares held by alleged nominees in the respondent company, with the interim receivers then-appointed applying for the appointment of provisional liquidators of the respondent company. In obtaining the initial receivership order, full and frank disclosure was given in respect of that application, but not in respect of the wider litigation strategy including the appointment of a provisional liquidator. At a subsequent hearing, Wallbank J discharged the receivership and provisional liquidation in part due to a lack of full and frank disclosure, explaining at [149] that:

> "*Where, as here, a receivership is to be the first part of a two-or multi-part remedy, then it makes perfect sense that the Court should be given as full and as balanced a view as possible of the merits of both or all parts of the remedy sought. That is because there would be no point, and indeed it would be contrary to principle, to grant one part of the remedy if another part has insufficient merit. This must be so where, as here, the remedies sought are interdependent. … Where, as here, an applicant has made it abundantly clear that he wishes to deploy a double-, or multiple-strike strategy using the Court's weapons, he comes under a duty to give full and frank disclosure and fair presentation of the whole plan.*"

Wherever fraud or dishonesty or related concepts are alleged, it is of course necessary to plead the basis of that wrongdoing with specificity – as to the acts relied on, the knowledge of the persons responsible, the duty that is said to have been breached, etc. As evidenced in the strike out of the dishonest assistance claim in *Stanford International Bank (in liquidation) v HSBC* [2021] 1 WLR 3507 (CA), adequately identifying and pleading the basic building blocks of a fraud case (including any alternative cases) is essential. The victim of an apparent fraud cannot rely on sympathy for their predicament as a substitute for proper pleadings.

Applicable law

The court is primarily obliged to apply the Rome I (concerned with contractual obligations) and Rome II (concerned with non-contractual obligations) regulations where it is necessary to establish the applicable law of any claims being brought in the jurisdiction. It is only where the subject matter of the claims made, such as trusts, fall outside the scope of these regulations that the court will consider other sources.

Art.3 of Rome I provides that a contract is governed by the law chosen, expressly or otherwise, by the parties. This is very likely to be the case with, for example, the claimant's contract with its bank or any counterparty.

Where there is no choice of law, Art.4 provides for various types of contract and identifies the applicable law for the same. For example, as may be relevant where a claim is made against an agent, Art.4(b) provides that "*a contract for the provision of services shall be governed by the law of the country where the service provider has his habitual residence*". All of the default rules are subject to the caveat that if the contract is manifestly more closely connected with some other jurisdiction, the law of that other jurisdiction applies.

Art.4 of Rome II provides that the applicable law for tort claims is the law of the jurisdiction where the damage occurred, unless both the claimant and defendant are habitually resident in the same jurisdiction or the tort is manifestly more closely connected with some other jurisdiction other than that of the loss or joint habitual residence of the parties.

Art.10 of Rome II provides that the applicable law for unjust enrichment claims is the law which governs the parties' relationship, alternatively the jurisdiction where both the claimant and defendant are habitually resident, otherwise the law of the jurisdiction where the enrichment took place. This is all subject to the caveat that if the claim is manifestly more closely connected with some other jurisdiction, then the law of that jurisdiction will apply.

Art.7 of the Hague Convention on the Recognition of Trusts (given effect by Recognition of Trusts Act 1987, *cf.* s.1(2)) provides that a trust shall, unless the settlor has chosen the applicable law, be governed by the law of the jurisdiction most closely connected with the trust, in respect of which "*reference shall be made in particular to*":

(a) the place of administration of the trust designated by the settlor;

(b) the *situs* of the assets of the trust;

(c) the place of residence or business of the trustee;

(d) the objects of the trust and the places where they are to be fulfilled.

Turning to each of the possible targets, as identified above:

<u>Fraudsters and accomplices:</u> The majority of claims against these classes of person are likely to be claims in tort. If so, these claims will probably be governed by the law of the jurisdiction where the money was stolen from, unless it is established that fraudsters and victim domiciled in same jurisdiction.

In international cyber fraud cases, it may be difficult to identify a 'manifestly most closely connected' jurisdiction unless the claimant had evidence of how the fraud was perpetrated (and potentially by whom). If the acts by which the fraud was perpetrated were substantially all committed in the jurisdiction then that may help establish a sufficient link with the jurisdiction to make the applicable law of the tort English law. If so, specific regard will have to be had to the constituent elements of the cause of action. For example, just because an English-domiciled actor obtained illicit access to the victim's English-based email server to perpetrate a fraud, that may not be sufficient to render England the most closely connected jurisdiction. The fraud may have been perpetrated as part of a grander conspiracy involving other persons and other wrongful actions, all of whom and all of whom or all of which may have been located in or perpetrated from the same foreign jurisdiction.

As for any trust claim (such as in respect of the traceable proceeds of the fraud), under the Hague Convention this would probably be governed by the jurisdiction where the trust was formed (i.e. where the traceable proceeds were received) or where the trust assets presently are. To similar, though not identical, effect, unjust enrichment claims would likely be governed by whatever jurisdiction the recipient of any traceable proceeds was enriched in.

Counterparties, agents, and claimant's own bank: These claims are likely to be contractual claims, alternatively claims in tort. The contractual claims will be governed by the law of the contract, which may well be expressly identified in the contract terms. If it is not, recourse will need to be had to Art.4 of Rome I to establish the applicable law. Where claims are made in tort, it may be that the parties' contract identifies the applicable law. If not, a claimant will need to identify the correct approach under Rome II.

Other third parties: The balance of a claimant's possible targets for action will likely be parties who have received the proceeds of the fraud or who have otherwise facilitated the fraud (but not knowingly, or otherwise not in such a manner as to render them liable as a fraudster or an accomplice). These claims will likely be limited to claims in tort, as to which the claimant will need to identify the applicable law by reference to Art.4 of Rome II.

Establishing jurisdiction against foreign defendants

Assuming that the claimant seeks to bring their claim in England or Wales against parties who are outside of that jurisdiction, the claimant may be required to seek permission to serve that claim on the intended defendants. Whether permission is required or not depends on whether the claimant can bring themselves within the scope of CPR 6.32 (service in Scotland or Northern Ireland) or r.6.33 (certain claims, e.g. made pursuant to the 2005 Hague Convention). If not, then permission is required.

In cases of cyber fraud, it is common that the claimant does not have certainty as to the location in which they will be required to serve the intended defendants. In particular, in cases where the claimant is bringing an action against persons unknown it is very likely that this will be the case. In these cases, the claimant would be well-advised to seek permission to serve out to ensure that the steps taken to serve the defendants with the claim form are not later declared to be ineffective.

Service of foreign defendants within the jurisdiction

The easiest way to achieve this is under CPR 6.32-33. Thus, for example, *Norwich Pharmacal* relief was granted in *Sabados v Facebook Ireland* [2018] EWHC 2369 (QB). This is despite the defendant being out of the jurisdiction (in Ireland) and the decision taking place after *AB Bank*. As explained above, *AB Bank* confirmed that permission could not – then – be granted to serve such claims out of the jurisdiction. Although *AB Bank* was not cited in *Sabados*, that would appear to be because it was not relevant (no permission being required).

There are additional cases where a foreign defendant has provided, for other purposes, an address within the jurisdiction which may be used for service.

First, where the foreign defendant is a registered officer of an English company, they are required to provide a correspondence address. Under s.1140 Companies Act 2006, an officer can be served at their correspondence address even in respect of matters unrelated to the company's business: *Brouwer v Anstey* [2019] EWHC 144 (Ch) at [30]-[32] (ICC Judge Jones). This will apply to both natural and corporate officers. In *Helice Leasing SAS v PT Garuda Indonesia (Persero) TbK* [2021] 1 Lloyd's Rep 395, it was held that a person could continue to be served at that address even after changing it, pending the change being given effect to.

Second, in the case of a foreign-domiciled company, it might have a registered UK establishment under s.1046 Companies Act 2006. This will typically be a branch of the company, which does not have separate legal personality, but is a place at which the foreign entity can be served within the jurisdiction: s.1139(2) Companies Act 2006; *Teekay Tankers Limited v STX Offshore & Shipping Co* [2014] EWHC 3612 (Comm).

Obtaining permission to serve out of the jurisdiction

When considering whether to grant permission to serve out, the English court is obliged to apply CPR 6.36, which requires the claimant to come within one of the 25 jurisdictional gateways set out in CPR

PD6B para.3.1. New gateways have recently been added to the list, in some cases as a direct response to the issues which arise in cyber fraud cases.

There are a number of gateways which are of particular interest in cyber fraud litigation:

First, an important jurisdictional gateway is gateway (3), which allows a claimant to join a third party outside of the jurisdiction where that third party is a necessary or proper party to a claim made by the claimant against a different defendant (who can be served other than in reliance on gateway (3)). This is particularly pertinent to claims for disclosure (under the *Norwich Pharmacal* or *Bankers Trust* jurisdictions) against parties such as banks, who may not otherwise be liable to the claimant. This directly engages with the issue, discussed above, as to whether banks and other third parties can be joined in these circumstances. In *AB Bank*, Teare J ruled that this gateway is not available in *Norwich Pharmacal* actions. However, the earlier case of *Mackinnon* suggests otherwise for *Bankers Trust* actions, at least (as recognised in *AB Bank*) exceptionally in cases which are excused "*by a commercial equivalent of hot pursuit*".

The court will scrutinise whether any particular claim can pass through the claimed gateway. In a recent case on alleged fraudulent misrepresentation, the court declined to allow service out under gateway (3) ('necessary and proper party' – the court found that the claim against the anchor defendant was capable of being summarily dismissed) or under gateway (9b) ('tortious acts committed in the jurisdiction' – the court found that the claimants were unable to demonstrate that "*substantial and efficacious acts*" were committed within the jurisdiction): *Manek v IIFL Wealth (UK) Ltd* [2019] EWHC 3361 (Comm).

Second, the new gateway (25) empowers the court to give permission to serve out to be granted where:

(25) A claim or application is made for disclosure in order to obtain information–

(a) regarding:

(i) the true identity of a defendant or a potential defendant; and/or

(ii) what has become of the property of a claimant or applicant; and

(b) the claim or application is made for the purpose of proceedings already commenced or which, subject to the content of the information received, are intended to be commenced whether by service in England and Wales or pursuant to CPR rule 6.32, 6.33 or 6.36.

This new rule is directly targeted at the issue identified in *AB Bank*, as discussed in an earlier section of this guide, discussing *Norwich* Pharmacal relief. However, the gateway is equally applicable to a claim for relief under the *Bankers Trust* jurisdiction or an application for pre-action or non-party disclosure. Indeed, it has already been used successfully in *LMN v Bitfly* [2022] EWHC 2954 (Comm) at [26] (relevant orders set out at [14]).

There are various important limits on this new gateway:

(1) It only enables claims to be made in respect of the narrow class of information expressly identified in subparagraph (a). It is not permitted, for example, to seek information to evidence the fact of wrongdoing having been committed, even if it is to identify the essential missing link in a claim which would then be ready to be pleaded. Information going to the 'true identity' of the defendant would probably include sufficient identifying details, such as their postal or email address.

(2) Where information beyond an intended defendant's identity is sought, it must relate to "*what has become of the property of a claimant or applicant*". Taking this in stages:

(a) It is therefore only concerned with activity subsequent to receipt, excluding (for example) any activity that took place on a bank account prior to receipt of the claimant's property, that prior activity being relevant for any backwards tracing claim that may be advanced.

(b) The concern with property, as opposed to former property, means that a proprietary claim must be advanced (i.e. this is concerned with the *Bankers Trust* jurisdiction rather than the broader *Norwich Pharmacal* jurisdiction).

(c) Moreover, the property must be that of the "*claimant or applicant*", who must therefore identify their personal proprietary interest in the property being traced. This may be especially relevant when investigating fraud in respect of crypto-assets, which may formally be held by – and thus owned by – an entity like an exchange, with the exchange's customer (who would be colloquially considered to be the 'owner' of the asset) having only a contractual right of control over the crypto-asset.

(3) The information sought must be for use only in claims served in this jurisdiction or under the CPR, so the gateway cannot be used to gather evidence for use in foreign proceedings (where it is necessary to seek permission to serve out) or, it would seem, in arbitration.

(4) The requirement that there be an intention to commence proceedings in the jurisdiction ensures that the gateway does not conflict with the decision in *Ramilos*. By analogy with the matters discussed above in respect of that decision (see the earlier section on *Norwich Pharmacal*), the intention requirement is likely to be set relatively low. It is likely to be met

if the claimant would be content to commence in the jurisdiction and did not have a reasonably certain intention to commence elsewhere instead.

Third, another new gateway is (1A): "*A claim is made against a person in respect of a dispute arising out of the operations of a branch, agency or other establishment of that person within the jurisdiction, but only if proceedings cannot be served on the branch, agency or establishment*".

This gateway allows a claimant to effect service on a local branch, with the Court's permission, even where the foreign entity has not registered a local establishment under s.1046 Companies Act 2006 (discussed above).

The new gateway is similar to Art.7(5) Brussels I (Recast) Regulations No 1215/2012, which has been interpreted as requiring "a place of business which has the appearance of permanency, such as the extension of a parent body, has a management and is materially equipped to negotiate business with third parties so that the latter, although knowing that there will if necessary be a legal link with the parent body, the head office of which is abroad, do not have to deal directly with such parent body but may transact business at the place of business constituting the extension": Case 33/78 *Somafer SA v Saar-Ferngas AG* [1978] ECR 2183 at [12].

The CJEU interpretation of Art.7(5) Brussels I poses a relatively high bar. Whether a similarly high threshold is policed by the English court will remain to be seen. In cases of fraud, the court has shown a willingness to exercise jurisdiction where justified. In *Credit Suisse Trust v Banca Monte Dei Paschi Di Siena* [2014] EWHC 1447 (Ch) at [12]-[14], HHJ Waksman QC allowed a claim for *Norwich Pharmacal* relief against an Italian bank where the case was plainly one of fraud and the information held by the Italian bank could be obtained by the actions of its English branch complying with the court's order. This case predates the decision in *AB Bank*, so its status as an authority permitting service out without permission is somewhat doubtful. However, it has recently been relied on in *A1 v R1* [2021] HKCFI 650 and does suggest that the court may be more liberal in its interpretation of the new gateway.

On a related note, if a "*control arrangement*" exists between a litigant and a third party, the litigant can be required to exercise that control and disclose the documents held by a third party: *Pipia v BGEO Group Ltd* [2020] EWHC 402 (Comm). If a foreign-domiciled disclosure target is subject to a 'control arrangement' by a person within the jurisdiction, it might be possible to seek a disclosure order against the person within the jurisdiction over documents within their control (i.e. including those held by the disclosure target). The point should not be taken too far, but in principle this could avoid the need for service out entirely.

Fourth, new gateways 15A & 15C have also been added to cover claims for unlawfully causing or assisting in a breach of trust, or unlawfully causing or assisting in a breach of fiduciary duty. Previously, such claims were required to pass through gateway (15) as claims "*made against the defendant as constructive trustee*".

Fifth, new gateways 23 is concerned with unlawfully causing or assisting in a breach of confidence or misuse of private information. This is another welcome addition, as more clearly providing a route to establish jurisdiction in cyber fraud cases.

Alternative and substituted service

The court has broad powers to permit service, both of process documents (i.e. claim forms and application notices) and other documents (e.g. evidence), by alternative methods or at alternative places where justified: e.g. CPR 6.15. The importance of ensuring that it is possible effectively and efficiently to serve defendants or respondents in cyber fraud cases should not be underestimated:

First, as explained by Lord Sumption in *Cameron v Liverpool Victoria Insurance Co Ltd* [2019] 1 WLR 1471 at [16], overcoming the conceptual difficulty of how to serve an anonymous person is probably a necessary step in enabling a victim of cyber fraud to bring proceedings against the fraudsters as 'persons unknown'.

Second, ensuring that the defendant or respondent in any particular instance is properly served is a threshold requirement before the court can proceed in certain circumstances – such as trial in the defendant's absence (discussed below) or on a return date for an *ex parte* application. Additionally, demonstrating that the defendant or respondent was properly served with the claim, application, notice of hearing, judgment or order is very likely to be a precondition to the claimant or applicant's ability to enforce any judgment or order made by the English court in other jurisdictions.

Third, in circumstances where time is of the essence, it may be necessary for the court to order service by an instantaneous method of service (such as by email) rather than a traditional method of service (such as by post to a foreign jurisdiction). In *AA v Persons Unknown* [2020] 4 WLR 35 at [77], alternative service by email was permitted against a crypto-currency exchange which had insisted on service by hard copy in the BVI on the basis that the service was of a proprietary injunction over crypto-assets within the exchange's control. The speed with which those assets could be moved, thus the urgency in preserving their current status, justified alternative service by email.

Fourth, alternative service provisions may significantly reduce the costs which the claimant will otherwise incur. For example, where a claimant is proceeding against a foreign-domiciled defendant, the claimant is required (absent a court order otherwise) to provide formal notice to the defendant of various matters. This may involve several rounds of service, such as in the situation where the claimant makes an *ex parte* application, is required to serve the order and application materials on the defendant, then is additionally required to serve that defendant with the return date application and various other materials.

Threshold for authorising alternative service

To authorise alternative or substituted service (whether prospectively or retrospectively), the court must be satisfied, on considering all the relevant circumstances, that there is a good reason for doing so. The court will consider the alternative method of service being proposed, together with the reason why the normal methods are insufficient. See *Société Générale v Goldas Kuyumculuk Sanayi* [2017] EWHC 667 (Comm) at [49] (confirmed on appeal: [2019] 1 WLR 346 (CA)). In considering whether to permit alternative service, the court will generally consider the extent to which the applicant has taken reasonable steps to effect service by conventional means: *Aslani v Taberna* [2021] EWHC 3631 (QB).

Lord Sumption in *Cameron* confirmed (at [21]) that "*it is an essential requirement for any form of alternative service that the mode of service should be such as can reasonably be expected to bring the proceedings to the attention of the defendant.*" See also *Canada Goose Retail v Persons Unknown* [2020] EWCA Civ 303 at [47]. This will inevitably be a factual question which the court will need to engage with on a case-by-case, and service method-by-service method, basis. The only exception to this requirement may be on public policy grounds in the case of certain statutory schemes.

There are additional considerations which apply when seeking alternative service orders in cases which would ordinarily require service pursuant to the Hague Convention: *Société Générale v Goldas* (HC) at [49(9)]. There are cases where alternative service orders have been set aside, with the effect that service was deemed not to have taken place, where these considerations are not adequately met: e.g. *Punjab National Bank v Boris Shipping* [2019] EWHC 1280 (QB).

In short, "*where the Hague Convention is a factor there will only be good reason if there are special circumstances*": *Russian Commercial Bank (Cyprus) Limited v Khoroshilov* [2020] EWHC 1164 (Comm) at [97] (Cockerill J). Absent such special circumstances, a party will be required to effect service in accordance with the Hague Service

Convention. It is not apparent that there is any distinction between 'special' and 'exceptional circumstances': *Koza v Akcil* [2018] EWHC 384 (Ch) at [48] (Richard Spearman QC).

A factor which may be of relevance in cyber fraud cases is that the court is prepared to treat the proper administration of justice as a sufficiently good reason. Thus, the first instance decisions in *Evison v Finvision* [2020] EWHC 239 (Comm) at [57]-[58] (Teare J) and *Avonwick Holdings Ltd v Azitio Holdings Ltd* [2019] EWHC 1254 (Comm) at [33]-[36] (Moulder J) suggest that alternative service can be granted notwithstanding the Hague Service Convention where to refuse to do so would involve significant delay in serving a party in circumstances where that delay would hold back proceedings that are already underway other parties to the litigation. This may be of assistance where one defendant is in a jurisdiction which has derogated from the non-mandatory elements of the Hague Service Convention, with the effect that service can only be completed through time-consuming judicial channels.

Methods of alternative service

The methods by which a court may be prepared to authorise the service of cyber fraudsters should not be considered to be a closed list. In considering applications for alternative service, the court is prepared to be flexible. As stated by HHJ Waksman QC in *CMOC v Persons Unknown* [2018] EWHC 2230 (Comm) at [190], "*the court will consider proactively different forms of alternative service where they can be justified in the particular case.*" Earlier in his judgment (at [188]), the judge referred to the "*need for the procedural armoury of the court to be sufficient to meet the challenges posed by the modern electronic methods of communication and of doing business.*"

In *CMOC*, the judge made a number of alternative disclosure orders. He stated (at [190]) that "*it is not uncommon where alternative modes of service are justified to find examples of service by posting the relevant materials on a public Facebook platform.*" He then referred to service by the Facebook Messenger service and by WhatsApp messenger. By analogy with Facebook, a claimant in an appropriate case might readily be able to justify service (whether by public post or private message) on various other social media channels, such as Twitter, LinkedIn, YouTube or Instagram.

The judge made reference to "*the particular virtue*" of WhatsApp being that the sender of a message can see whether and when it has been both delivered to the recipient's device and subsequently accessed by a device-user. This feature is not unique to WhatsApp and has the potential, at least, to give a judge proceeding in the absence of a defendant or respondent the additional comfort that someone with access to the recipient's device or passcode has received or read the message by which service was effected.

That said, there is a concern as to the propriety of the serving party having access to this information – certainly if the information extended to identifying who had accessed the message. Traditionally, with service by post for example, the serving party had no means of knowing if or when the served party read the message. Such information was not relevant. That said, the Court of Appeal was not concerned about parties requiring proof of actual delivery and the identity of the recipient in cases of ordinary post: *Diriye v Bojaj* [2020] EWCA Civ 1400. However, consider the situation where a new digital method of service reported back to the serving party the email address of the party who had accessed a document via a weblink. Such information could enable a serving party to discover whether, for example, the party being served had instructed legal representatives if those representatives accessed the link directly (bringing into play consideration in *Loreley Financing (Jersey) No 30 Ltd v Credit Suisse Securities (Europe) Ltd* [2022] EWCA Civ 1484, where the question was whether the identity of the person instructing lawyers was privileged information).

In any event, it is not necessary that the recipient (or anyone else) actually see the relevant message. In a somewhat different context, it has been held that a notice failing to come to the recipient's attention due to it being automatically filtered into his junk email folder was not a relevant consideration, it being that recipient's responsibility to check his junk email folder (and his failure to so check being "*unreasonable*"): *R (Mumim) v Secretary of State for the Home Department* [2020] EWCA Civ 49 at [11], [20] & [22(ii)-(iii)] (Hickinbottom LJ).

It is important to be precise in describing the alternative service method and what is sufficient to constitute good service. By way of analogy, a tax tribunal recently held that the contents of an email had not been adequately lodged where the email was sent but had not been received by the tribunal. Even though the email may have reached the recipient's email server, the fact that it was not delivered to the recipient (potentially due to the email firewall settings which imposed a limit on the size of attachments which could be received) was sufficient to prevent it from being served: *Ashfield v HMRC* [2020] UKFTT 0110 (TC) at [6]-[15] (Judge Gillet). An applicant would be well-advised to ensure that the wording of the alternative service order only requires an effective outgoing transmission, not also requiring effecting incoming receipt by the service target (which matter may be outside of the applicant's control).

The judge in *CMOC* (at [191]) also described a further novel method of service permitted in that case:-

> which involved sending the relevant party by a previously approved Court method (e.g. email or hard copy) a link to a data room, and by a separate email, an access code to the data room. If the code was used, it would enable the user to view all of the evidence thus far adduced together with all applications and orders made.

Service via data room has since been employed in other jurisdictions. In *Hwang Joon Sang v Golden Electronics* [2020] HKCFI 1084, Coleman J allowed the approach in *CMOC* to be used in Hong Kong, commenting at [36]:

> In some ways, the provision of the link to the data room might be regarded as akin to an envelope or package containing documents, and the access code or password to use the link akin to the method

> by which to open the envelope or package. Clearly, the link and the access code together will provide ready access to the documentation in a form which many, if not most, would find more convenient than hardcopy. It would do so in a way which is quick, efficient, and cost-effective – and also relatively secure.

In the specific case of assets recorded on the blockchain, there is the option in some cases of airdropping a token to a particular wallet, which has been approved as an alternative service procedure in a small number of cases: e.g. *D'Aloia v Persons Unknown* [2022] EWHC 1723 (Ch); *Jones v Persons Unknown* [2022] EWHC 2543 (Comm). This shows a tension in the purpose and effect of service, and airdrop service is likely to remain the exception rather than the rule. Where the wallet address is associated with an exchange or other entity, it may well be possible to obtain contact details (e.g. an email address) of the wallet holder. A freezing injunction, for example, can then be served by email, both on the wallet holder and on the exchange (who will – it is hoped – assist in its enforcement). This is the preferred option for service.

Where the wallet address is not associated with a known third party, such that the wallet holder is entirely unknown, providing documents by a 'service token' will tip the wallet holder off without the litigant having any means of enforcing compliance by the wallet holder. The public nature of the record on the blockchain could in theory tip off other wrongdoers who are not yet known to exist. The reason for taking the airdrop approach to service will be where there is no better method of service, though in that case it may be prudent not to seek a freezing injunction or similar but to monitor transactions in the hope that the assets are moved to a more accessible location.

Dispensing with service

In exceptional circumstances, the court additionally has the power to dispense with the claimant's obligation to serve documents on the defendant: e.g. CPR 6.16. As observed in *Cameron* (at [25], emphasis added), the CPR 6.16 power:

> has been exercised on a number of occasions and considered on many more. In general, these have been cases in which the claimant has sought to invoke CPR r 6.16 in order to escape the consequences of some procedural mishap in the course of attempting to serve the claim form by one of the specified methods, or to confer priority on the English court over another forum for the purpose of the Brussels Regulation, or to affect the operation of a relevant limitation period. In all of them, the defendant or his agents was in fact aware of the proceedings, generally because of a previous attempt by the claimant to serve them in a manner not authorised by the Rules. … I would accept that it may be appropriate to dispense with service, even where no attempt has been made to effect it in whatever manner, if the defendant has deliberately evaded service and cannot be reached by way of alternative service under CPR r 6.15 . This would include cases where the defendant is unidentifiable but has concealed his identity in order to evade service. However, a person cannot be said to evade service unless, at a minimum, he actually knows that proceedings have been or are likely to be brought against him. A court would have to be satisfied of that before it could dispense with service on that basis. … But the court cannot deny him [i.e. the defendant] an opportunity to be heard simply because it thinks it inherently improbable that he would take advantage of it.

Lord Sumption's comments were applied in *Canada Goose Retail v Persons Unknown* [2020] EWCA Civ 303 at [51]-[52], where the Court of Appeal refused to dispense with service notwithstanding the claimant's submissions that 121 persons had already been served with the order and that the terms were likely to be known by a far larger class of protestors.

A claimant would be advised to seek dispensation of service only where absolutely necessary. Wherever possible, a sensible method of alternative or substituted service should be sought – even if the success of the same is not guaranteed:

First, a claimant will encounter great difficulty in seeking to dispense with service. It is far from obvious that a perpetrator of a cyber fraud "*actually knows that proceedings... are likely to be brought against him*" without more. As an illustration of the sort of exceptional circumstances which the court will look for under CPR 6.16, it is instructive to consider *Lonestar Communications Corp LLC v Kaye* [2019] EWHC 3008 (Comm) as a cyber fraud case in which dispensation was recently granted where one perpetrator sought to evade service in the face of "*heroic*" attempts being made by the claimant to contact him. The judge was satisfied on the evidence that the unserved defendant must have become aware of the proceedings, since he had (for example) suspended a Facebook messenger account when the claimant sought to contact him by those means.

Second, there is an enforcement concern. The fact that the English court has dispensed with the need to serve a particular document may not carry any weight when the claimant seeks to enforce the subsequent judgment or order in another jurisdiction, with the judge in that other jurisdiction considering an argument by the defendant that the judge should refuse to enforce the English judgment or order because of a failure by the claimant to effect proper service.

As a footnote to this discussion, in *LJY v Persons Unknown* [2018] EMLR 19 an unusual form of alternative service order was made. There, the persons unknown could only be reliably contacted by text message for a period of 4 days. It was ordered that after the expiry of that period (and provided that the defendants had not self-identified, as ordered to do by an injunction served by text message) then service on them would be deemed to have taken place by the filing of the Claim Form and Particulars of Claim at the court: at [53]-[56]. The judgment does not record the procedural basis for this form of 'alternative' service, which in truth seems to be a dispensation with the need to serve. Although an equivalent approach has since been taken in *AA v Persons Unknown* [2020] 4 WLR 35 at [75], litigants would be well-advised to take this approach only in the most extreme cases such as where no other means of possible service can be identified.

Non-disclosure orders

In cyber fraud proceedings, particularly at the early stages, it is not uncommon to see non-disclosure provisions (sometimes colloquially referred to as 'gagging orders') included in orders. It is notable that this is perhaps the main residual use of what have previously been termed 'super-injunctions' – i.e. injunctions which not only require or preclude certain actions by the respondent, but which also preclude the respondent from notifying third parties that the injunction exists.

The most common use of non-disclosure orders (NDOs) in cyber fraud litigation is to prevent one fraudster, who has been notified of the proceedings or a court order, from disclosing the same to other parties to the fraud. For this reason, a claimant who has brought proceedings against persons unknown to recover a fraudulent payment may wish to include NDOs in the initial (and potentially subsequent) freezing and disclosure orders. These NDOs would provide that a respondent who has notice of the order being served (including the NDO) is not to disclose to third parties either the existence of the order or the nature or contents of the application materials which formed part of the evidence in support of the order. The benefit to such a claimant is, for example, that it prevents an early-served respondent from tipping off a co-respondent to the freezing injunction, which has not yet been served (and is thus not yet effective) on the co-respondent. This mitigates the risk of one fraudster, served with the order, notifying their co-conspirators of the status of the claimant's asset tracing exercise and thereby enabling the fraudsters as a whole to dissipate any assets which are at risk of discovery or seizure.

The serious nature of NDOs must be appreciated. The sanction for breach of an NDO potentially very severe, as it allows an applicant to bring committal proceedings against the subject for contempt of court. Given that an NDO is an inevitable restriction of the right to free speech, the grant of an NDO is required to meet an elevated threshold rather than the simple *American Cyanamid* test: s.12(3) Human Rights Act 1998. A claimant must therefore demonstrate either: (a) that the respondent, unless restrained, was likely to disclose the information which the NDO seeks to restrict; or (b) that the potential harm which would follow if the respondent disclosed the information was "*particularly grave*": *Cream Holdings Ltd v Banerjee* [2005] 1 AC 253 at [22] (Lord Nicholls). As a recent example, in *UKIP v Braine* [2019] EWHC 3527 (QB), the applicant obtained an interim NDO. However, the court dismissed the application to continue the NDO on the basis that only the *American Cyanamid* test was met, not the elevated test required by s.12(3), and the applicant was criticised for failing to bring that elevated test to the court's attention at the initial application. Regard may also be had to the Master of the Rolls' Practice Guidance: Interim Non-Disclosure Orders at [4]-[7].

For this reason, NDOs must be clearly justified on the evidence. The courts will be careful not to restrict a respondent's right to free speech unless persuaded that to do so is proportionate – both generally, but also on the particular terms sought. Thus, for example, the NDO might be limited in time or only apply to certain information or materials. Alternatively, the NDO might provide that the respondent is not to disclose information to certain individuals, rather than (as is more common) providing that the respondent is not to disclose information to anyone save as specifically permitted by the NDO.

One such specific permission is the necessary exception in the NDO which allows the respondent to disclose the relevant materials to their legal (and possibly other professional) advisers. Generally, a court will be very slow to cut down this exception. However, if there is a specific and well-evidenced concern that the respondent will instruct advisers who are party to the fraud or otherwise considered likely to notify other fraudsters of the injunction, thought will have to be given to how this risk is dealt with – for example, by restricting the respondent's choice of advisers, or by providing in the order that the advisers are also to be made subject to an NDO.

In the case of cyber fraud, the elevated test can readily be met in certain circumstances. For example, where there is a good arguable case that a conspiracy to perpetrate a fraud has been carried out, the court is likely to accept that one conspirator served with a freezing injunction (for example) might inform their co-conspirators before those co-conspirators are served. It might also be said that cases of fraud are more likely to involve sufficiently serious consequences if disclosure does take place, as it will likely involve further steps taken by the wrongdoers to dissipate the proceeds of the fraud and to destroy any evidence of the wrongdoing.

It is important to also recognise the limitations of NDOs:

First, it relies on the party who is made subject to the NDO complying with that NDO. The concept of a law-abiding fraudster is perhaps a contradiction in terms, but a fraudster who has been caught – or who only formed a relatively minor part of the fraud – may be more inclined to obey court orders once in place. Although the court should not make orders which it does not consider will serve any purpose, the court should equally not go too far in assuming that respondents will simply ignore otherwise useful orders. Alternatively, if the NDO is not complied with, that is an unlawful act which the claimant can rely on as part of its claims for damages – such as for unlawful means conspiracy.

Second, the NDO may not be enforceable in other jurisdictions. NDOs are a serious form of relief which many jurisdictions do not recognise or grant. This undoubtedly is a strength of proceeding in England & Wales, but with cyber fraud often being international in nature it is necessary to consider how the court's order including an NDO will be received in foreign jurisdictions should a claimant need to enforce the order there. It is possible that the foreign court will simply refuse to give to the NDO part of the order, alternatively there is a risk that the foreign court will consider itself entitled not to give effect to the order as a whole due to part of the order being contrary to local law. Applicants would be well advised to seek local law advice in any jurisdictions in which they consider it particularly likely that recognition or enforcement of court orders will be required.

For further guidance on NDOs, reference may be made to the Master of the Rolls' Practice Guidance: Interim Non-Disclosure Orders.

Proceeding in private

It is common for an initial application in cyber fraud cases, and for subsequent applications where appropriate, to be heard in private under CPR 39.2(1)-(3). A hearing must be held publicly unless one of a number of justifications is engaged, such that the court considers that privacy is necessary. This is a high threshold.

The most commonly deployed justification in this context is that "*publicity would defeat the object of the hearing*": CPR 39.2(3)(a). This is particularly relevant in early disclosure applications to trace assets, or subsequently to obtain freezing injunctions over them. An applicant may be concerned that there is a real risk that a public application would come to the attention of fraudsters.

If the matter is heard in private, CPR 39.2(5) provides that any order made at the private hearing is to be published on the Judiciary website, "*Unless and to the extent that the court otherwise directs*". For the same reason as a private hearing is justified, it may also be justified to seek a direction that the publication is not to take place for a certain period.

As an alternative privacy protection, and one that does not require a delay to the publication of orders made in private, the applicant could seek an order that their identity be kept secret – i.e. anonymisation of the proceedings. CPR 39.2(4) again imposes a strict condition that the anonymity must be "*necessary to secure the proper administration of justice and in order to protect the interests of that person.*" This is less of an incursion into the open justice principle than absolute secrecy.

In addition or as an alternative to these protections, applicants may wish to apply for access to the court file to be restricted. The court's power to do so is in CPR 5.4C. Without imposing restrictions, third parties can obtain statements of case from the court office, and could apply to the court (not necessarily on notice to the applicant) to receive other documents such as witness statements. Regard should be had as to whether the purpose sought to be achieved can be met if only certain documents (rather than the entirety of the court file) is subject to restricted access. It is also necessary to address the confidentiality of any hearing bundles which are produced. A template order is in the Master of the Rolls' Practice Guidance: Interim Non-Disclosure Orders.

As an illustration of these steps being taken in an extortion case, see *PML* at [5] & [14]-[16]. To do otherwise may defeat the very purpose of seeking to restrain the blackmailer. For example, if the victim wishes to avoid publicity surrounding the breach of its cyber security, publicly naming the victim in court would be much the same as the blackmailer carrying through the threat. Conducting hearings (or at least reviewing specific evidence) in private may also be defensible on basis that where (as in *PML*) confidential information is published online, it is necessary for the location of that published information to be kept private pending its removal following the hearing, as otherwise the purpose behind the court's order would be frustrated.

For a wrongful payment case and tracing exercise, see *AA* at [20]-[33] & [36]. There, Bryan J confirmed that the same principles applied as in an extortion case. Further, in addition to reacting to the danger of tipping off the fraudsters as to the claimant's investigation and tracing efforts, Bryan J considered a relevant factor being retaliatory cyber attacks upon both the direct victim of the fraud (whose crypto-assets were misappropriated) and the victim's insurer (who brought the proceedings as a subrogated claim).

Obtaining judgment

In instances of cyber fraud, the victim's most-pressing concern is often to seek immediate relief, whether this be a freezing injunction in respect of misappropriated property or an interim restraint on publication of information in extortion cases. However, once any interim relief is obtained, the victim's concern will turn to relief in the longer term. This may be in the form of a proprietary order, damages or permanent (or at least long-term) injunctive relief (or a combination of the above).

Cyber fraudsters will commonly not contest or otherwise engage with legal proceedings issued by the victim. If so, the claimant-victim has the option of seeking default judgment on its claim pursuant to CPR Part 12. This has the benefit of obtaining a judgment swiftly and at relatively little cost. Default judgment was ordered in a fraudulent payment case, where the claimant had successfully frozen certain misappropriated sums and the cyber fraudster (who had subsequently been identified) did not engage: *World Proteins KFT v Persons Unknown* [2019] EWHC 2030 (QB).

There are two caveats to be considered before seeking default judgment in cases of cyber fraud:

First, the relief being sought is often not confined to a claim for a specified sum of money. Frequently, a declaration (e.g. as to a proprietary interest) or injunctive relief (e.g. restraining future conduct) is sought. In such cases, the claimant is required by CPR 12.4 to make an CPR Part 23 application, rather than merely file a request. Further, "*declarations should not be given [on default judgment] without argument* inter partes, *save in the clearest cases.*": *Goldcrest Distribution Ltd v McCole* [2016] EWHC 1571 (Ch) at [43] (Master Matthews).

Second, default judgment is at the greatest risk of subsequently being overturned or otherwise rendered unenforceable by the defendant. As compared with the other options to be considered, below, the threshold for the defendant to set aside default judgment pursuant to CPR Part 13 is relatively low. Further, and perhaps more pertinently in cases of international cyber fraud, not all jurisdictions will recognise and enforce a default judgment. Thus, where the claimant wishes to claim assets in foreign jurisdictions, consideration should be given to whether those jurisdictions would be likely to support an English default judgment.

An alternative to seeking default judgment is for the claimant to apply for summary judgment pursuant to CPR Part 24. In circumstances where default judgment is being sought on a claim for relief other than the payment of a specified sum, an application for summary judgment is unlikely to incur significantly increased costs. However, a claimant needs to be aware that it needs the court's permission to make a summary judgment application if the defendant has not filed either an acknowledgement of service or a defence (CPR 24.4(1)), albeit that the claimant can apply for this permission at the same time as applying for summary judgment (*F BN Bank v Leaf Tobacco A Michailides SA* [2017] EWHC 3017 (Comm) and *EU v The Syrian Arab Republic* [2018] EWHC 1712 (Comm)). Where the claimant has sought interim relief of some sort (such as a freezing order, non-disclosure order, or similar) and does not anticipate engagement by the defendant, it is common that the continuation of the interim relief includes a provision that the Claimant be required to take steps to conclude the action (such as by default or summary judgment: *cf. PML v Persons Unknown* [2018] EWHC 838 (QB) at [11] & [19]), which may (depending on the precise terms of the order) be a sufficient permission for these purposes.

Where the defendant has engaged with or contested the claim, albeit in such a way that the defendant's defence has no real prospect of success, the summary judgment procedure is the only way to sensibly dispose of the defence without proceeding to trial.

A material benefit is that it is more difficult for a defendant later to set aside summary judgment within this jurisdiction. Further, it may be that summary judgment process (which requires the court to make an assessment of the merits of the claimant's claim) is more likely to be enforced in certain foreign jurisdictions.

On this latter point, it would be prudent for the claimant to seek local law advice in jurisdictions where the claimant contemplates bringing enforcement proceedings. For example, where misappropriated property has been transferred to Hong Kong, the claimant should seek Hong Kong law advice on whether the Hong Kong court would allow the claimant to rely on the English summary judgment to obtain a Hong Kong order for repossession of the misappropriated property. Hong Kong is mentioned as an example for two reasons. First, cyber fraudsters have frequently laundered the proceeds of fraud though Hong Kong and other offshore jurisdictions. Second, Hong Kong law previously prohibited parties from seeking summary judgment in Hong

Kong on any issue which involves an allegation of dishonesty or deception, irrespective of the apparent merits of such allegation: *Zimmer Sweden AB v KPN Hong Kong Ltd* [2016] 1 HKLRD 1016. This prohibition has since been lifted, but the extent to which it remains a relevant factor when seeking to enforce a foreign judgment remains a point of uncertainty.

Otherwise, the claimant will need to pursue a full judgment following the trial of its claim. This will require the claimant to go through all of the normal procedural steps, incurring the concomitant additional expense, to prepare for trial – even if, as discussed above, the defendant does not attend or engage. In cases of cyber fraud, this route will probably only be required where either: (a) one or more defendants properly engage with the claim and dispute liability on a substantive basis; or (b) the claimant is concerned about the prospects of enforcing abroad anything less than a full merits judgment.

If the matter is to proceed to a full judgment, particularly if the defendants are not engaging and the main purpose of the trial is to maximise the enforceability of any judgment, the claimant will wish to give careful consideration to the procedure necessary to bring the matter to trial. The directions to trial will set out the procedural steps required, each of which will entail cost to the claimant. The claimant will therefore wish to ensure that the directions (such as those addressing disclosure obligations) are not unduly burdensome. The court will likely be accommodating to a claimant in these circumstances who wishes to ensure that the procedure to trial is proportionate in the circumstances. The claimant may wish to have regard to the options provided by the pilot schemes for Shorter Trials and Flexible Trials provided for by CPR PD 57AB.

Trial in the absence of a party

Where a hearing (whether a trial or an interim hearing: *Hirbodan Management Co v Cummins Power Generation Ltd* [2021] EWHC 3315 (Comm)) is not attended by one of the litigating parties, the party which is represented is subject to an obligation of fair presentation. This obligation is not as stringent as the duty of full and frank disclosure in without notice hearings, but does – as the name indicates – require the represented party fairly to present the issues to the court, given that the court is not able to rely on the non-attending party's representative bringing opposing points to the court's attention.

In *Braspetro Oil Services v FPSO Construction Inc* [2007] EWHC 1359 (Comm) at [32]-[38], Cresswell J provided some guidance on fair presentation, which may be summarised as follows:

(1) The represented party is to draw to the court's attention factual or legal points which the non-attending party might benefit from. This should include any points which the non-attending party has previously raised (e.g. in correspondence), as well as further points which occur to the represented party as points which the non-attending party might have taken had attended.

(2) The represented party should only pursue claims which it is wholly satisfied are valid. Other claims should not be pursued at trial.

(3) The represented party is to take all practicable steps to bring to the non-attending party's attention all relevant events within the proceedings. This should include properly serving the non-attending party with any claim form, statements of case, notice of the trial date, any skeleton argument or written submissions and (following trial) notice of the judgment date.

Even with these considerations in mind, the court will be careful to carefully examine and test the represented party's case.

In cases where final relief in the form of non-disclosure orders (NDOs) is sought, the court is required by s.12 Human Rights Act 1998 not to proceed in the defendant's absence unless "*(a) the applicant has taken all reasonable steps to notify the respondent; or (b) that there are compelling reasons why the respondent should not be notified.*": *Pirtek (UK) v Jackson*

[2017] EWHC 2834 (QB) at [19]-[24] (Warby J). s.12(a) is a legislative basis for *Braspetro* step (3).

The court will also be cautious about proceeding in the absence of a party where that party expresses a wish to attend. In *RP Explorer Ltd v Malhotra* [2020] EWHC 1225 (Comm), the defendant was in prison and applied shortly before the trial for an adjournment, so that he could instruct lawyers and attend. The claimant was unable to persuade the court to refuse the application, which was adjourned for further consideration (albeit without reference to CPR 3.1(2)(b)).

Post-judgment orders

Where a claimant has pursued a cyber fraudster through to judgment, it is likely that they will have sought and obtained an interim freezing injunction over the defendant's assets. Assuming that they are confirmed on the return date following the initial *ex parte* application, such orders are commonly ordered to persist until judgment or further order of the court. Thus, absent further action by the claimant, they will lose the benefit of interim freezing injunctions at the same time that they receive the judgment (hopefully in the claimant's favour and which the claimant probably intends to enforce against the defendant's hitherto frozen assets).

In cases such as this, the claimant will generally wish formally to apply for post-judgment freezing injunctions, continuing the effect of the earlier interim orders beyond judgment. Post-judgment freezing injunctions are commonly expressed to operate until full satisfaction of the judgment debt or further order of the court.

Post-judgment freezing orders are more readily granted than pre-judgment orders. This is explicable on the basis that the claimant now has a judgment in their favour and an entitlement to be paid by the defendant (albeit not necessarily out of the frozen assets), rather than merely having a good arguable case. Indeed, a claimant may be entitled to post-judgment freezing injunctions even if they did not apply for or were not granted interim freezing injunctions. A claimant may also be entitled to join third parties anew where, for example, there is evidence that the defendant intends to use those third parties to avoid paying the judgment debt: *New York Laser Clinic Ltd v Naturastudios Ltd* (unreported, 15 November 2019).

The Court of Appeal has recently given some guidance on post-judgment freezing injunctions in two separate cases:

First, in *Lakatamia Shipping v Morimoto* [2019] EWCA Civ 2203, the court set out guidance on the circumstances in which a respondent's past conduct can be said to be evidence of a current risk of dissipation. This may be particularly relevant in cases of cyber fraud, where the fraudster has subsequently engaged with proceedings but where the claimant (having prevailed on at least some causes of action) is concerned that the respondent's previous misdemeanours indicate a propensity to evade enforcement.

Second, in *Michael Wilson v Emmott* [2019] EWCA Civ 219, the court considered the purpose and terms of post-judgment freezing injunctions. Among other matters, the court confirmed that the mere fact that the injunction was sought to encourage the respondent to satisfy the judgment debt did not necessarily make the order an illegitimate one to seek if the relevant criteria for an order were otherwise satisfied. The court also explained that there was not a presumption (unlike in applications for interim orders) that the respondent was entitled to use the otherwise-frozen assets in the ordinary course of business. The court stated that there was not a presumption that this exception would not be included, only that it had to be determined on the facts in each case; removal of the exception was expressly said not to be a remedy of last resort

For completeness, similar points may be made in respect of post-judgment proprietary injunctions.

Enforcement

As has been touched on in the previous section on obtaining judgment, it is important in cyber fraud cases (particularly where defendants and respondents may not engage with the proceedings) to ensure that any interim and final orders obtained are enforceable in whatever jurisdiction the claimant wishes to take those orders to. It would be a pyrrhic victory for a claimant to obtain an English judgment in a cyber fraud case, but when the claimant seeks to enforce that judgment against a foreign-domiciled fraudster the local courts refuse to give effect to the judgment.

Plainly, whether or not a judgment or order of the English court can be enforced in other jurisdictions is a question for the law of the jurisdiction in which that judgment or order is to be enforced. A claimant should therefore seek local law advice on whether there are any specific requirements imposed by the law of likely enforcement jurisdictions. However, by way of general guidance, it would be prudent for the claimant to be scrupulous in its compliance with the procedural (and particularly service) requirements of the English court. Issues of service and proceeding in the absence of the defendant are addressed above. Similarly, the desideratum of scrupulous compliance emphasises the importance of the claimant giving careful consideration to the terms of any proposed directions to trial, as discussed above.

A specific note on the enforcement of freezing injunctions: a claimant who applies for and obtains a freezing injunction will generally be required to seek the court's express permission before seeking to enforce that order in other jurisdictions (a process sometimes referred to as the 'domestication' of the English order). An applicant for a freezing injunction is expected to use the standard form of wording for freezing injunctions when making its application. Paragraph 10 of schedule B to this standard form provides that:

> The Applicant will not without the permission of the Court seek to enforce this order in any country outside England and Wales [or

seek an order of a similar nature including orders conferring a charge or other security against the Respondent or the Respondent's assets].

The purpose of this undertaking is to protect the respondent from a multiplicity of suits in numerous jurisdictions, to ensure that the applicant does not obtain security or *quasi*-security in other jurisdictions, and to protect the interests of third parties: *Derby & Co v Weldon* [1990] Ch 48 (CA). The court has a discretion as to the circumstances in which it will give permission to enforce a freezing injunction abroad. In exercising this discretion, the court will refer to the guidelines identified in *Dadourian Group International v Simms* [2006] 1 WLR 2499 (CA) at [25] (Arden LJ).

In cases of international cyber fraud, speed is often of the essence. Assets may be quickly and frequently dispersed from one jurisdiction to another. Such circumstances may weigh heavily in the court's assessment of whether the grant of permission will be just and convenient. It is therefore possible that the courts will consider granting broad *Dadourian* permission to the victim of a cyber fraud, enabling the victim (i.e. the applicant) to take swift action abroad to achieve the purpose of the freezing injunction. However, this broad permission must be contingent on the applicant satisfying the court that the underlying purposes of the standard undertaking (as identified in *Derby & Co*) will be achieved by suitable further protections, to be included as a condition of the *Dadourian* permission being granted: *cf. Arcadia Petroleum Ltd v Bosworth* [2015] EWHC 3700 (Comm). What further protections are sufficient will inevitably be a context-sensitive matter which will vary from case to case.

CHAPTER EIGHT

CODA ON FUTURE DEVELOPMENTS

In this guide, occasional references are made as to how the legal landscape might change as cyber fraud litigation becomes more prevalent. Most of these changes are incremental in nature, it being harder to predict with any confidence the more dramatic shifts which may take place. That caveat in place, this chapter indulges in some crystal ball-gazing with a view to highlighting some possible areas for development.

Legal developments

First, the Law Commission has been highly engaged in issues relevant to cyber fraud. The Commission previously published a report on 'Smart contracts', and currently has a number of other projects at pre-consultation or policy development stages – namely, 'Digital assets', 'Digital assets: which law, which court?' (previously 'Conflict of laws and emerging technology') and 'Decentralised Autonomous Organisations'.

The outcome of these reports may have a significant effect on cyber fraud litigation. Most immediately and notably, if the Law Commission's proposal that a new category of property be created for digital assets such as crypto-assets, then this will have a direct bearing in any cyber fraud case involving such assets.

However, other matters, such as the nature of DAOs and the means by which knowledge may be attributed to such supposed entities could have significant ramifications. Lord Briggs has previously observed that "*The court is well versed in identifying the governing mind of a corporation, and, when the time arises, will no doubt be able to do the same for robots*": *Warner-Lambert Co Ltd v Generics (UK) Ltd* [2019] 3 All ER 95 (SC) at [165]. What goes for robots in this regard will also go for DAOs. Indeed, in an early foray into an analogous area, the Singapore court in *B2C2 v Quoine* [2019] SGHC(I) 03 (on appeal, [2020] SGCA(I) 02) attributed the knowledge of a code programmer to the parties when the parties subsequently contracted on terms set by the code.

Proceeding against fraudsters

Second, a significant obstacle in present cyber fraud litigation is in the economic viability (or otherwise) of proceeding against anonymous fraudsters who only operate online. Many victims will not approach lawyers, those that do may only do so belatedly – possibly after making contact with Action Fraud (a joint operation run by the City of London Police working alongside the National Fraud Intelligence Bureau, recently criticised by government reports, but due to be revitalised with assistance from the National Cyber Security Centre). Those victims who do contact lawyers may then decide against issuing proceedings, given the relatively high cost of commencing proceedings compared with the relatively low likelihood of directly engaging the fraudsters (or their assets) in litigation.

There are two possible solutions to this. On the one hand, the victim can look to other more visible targets. Their ability to do so is somewhat limited and discussed in this guide, though areas such as the voluntary banking code may provide some additional recourse going forwards. The other solution is to reduce the economic hurdle facing victims (and prospective litigants) in cases of cyber fraud.

The reduction in the economic hurdle may be achieved by cooperation between various stakeholders, such as Members of Parliament, criminal law enforcement authorities, lawyers and litigation funders. Various models might result.

One option would be for a victim of a fraudulent payment scheme who contacts Action Fraud to opt into their details being referred on to an identified scheme. This scheme will be engaged where the public law enforcement authorities consider that the victim's case is not in the public interest to investigate (often on the basis that costs of doing so are disproportionate). In such cases, the victim may be referred to a law firm or a litigation funder for consideration. It may be that a protocol, or at least a template, can be established which makes it easier and cheaper for claims to be commenced against fraudsters. Doing so will reduce the entry barrier to commencement, and (subject to terms) may result in a funder (rather than an individual victim) taking the initial risk of commencing proceedings without any guaranteed return. In the absence of anything more formal, it may simply be that an asset recovery firm or funder experienced in this form of litigation may take an assignment of victims' claims in exchange for the victim receiving a guaranteed payment in respect of the fraud from the firm or funder.

Alternatively, rather than civil lawyers and a funder stepping in when the prosecuting authority steps away, the two factions can work in tandem. The investigating authority could share in the initial or subsequent risk alongside a funder and the victim, with the policy decision being that this – the recovery of stolen property and the investigation of fraud – would be an appropriate use of government funding.

A yet further possibility is that individual victims collectively share the initial risk in proceeding against the unknown fraudsters. An appropriate data management process would have to be put in place to ensure that individual victims' data (e.g. bank account details) are stored and processed in a suitable manner. However, it is possible that links could be drawn between different individuals who appear to have fallen victim to the same unknown fraudster – e.g. by working on the *prima facie* basis that misappropriated payments channelled through the same account are part of a wider organised network of fraudsters. These linked individuals could commence proceedings together. This may simply take the form of being joint claimants, or it could involve a Group Litigation Order under CPR Part 19.

At the very least, in the absence of a more organised framework, grouped claimants might represent a more attractive proposition to litigation funders. Equally, it must be recognised that this would likely require an efficient means of collating and processing information from victims, and there is the ever-present risk of recovery becoming more unlikely and expensive the longer that a fraudster is allowed to remain in possession of (and potentially dissipate) the proceeds of the fraud. Regard will need to be had to the Supreme Court's ruling in *Lloyd v Google* [2021] UKSC 50. Although the court broadly encouraged the use of representative actions where appropriate, one significant factor which precluded such proceedings was where there is the need to engage in individualised assessment – likely all but inevitable in cases of cyber fraud, where the claim is concerned with the recovery of lost assets.

The appetite of insurance firms to engage in this sort of process may also be relevant. Many insurance products are currently available to guard individuals and businesses against the risk posed by cyber fraud. Lloyd's of London has recently announced a specific policy to protect against losses arising from theft of crypto-assets held in online wallets. It may be that insurance companies currently take the view that pursuing the fraudsters themselves, after the insurer pays out under their customers' policies, is not a cost-effective approach to take. However, if the process becomes easier or if the fraud is large enough to warrant it, this may change.

Third, increased visibility of this sort of fraud may assist both to reduce its incidence (through education) and to assist in recovery actions (through knowledge sharing). The second element has partly been discussed above, but these changes may also be prompted by new regulation:

EU regulations such as the Network Information Security Directive (commonly referred to as the NIS Directive) and the Global Data Protection Regulations already require certain entities to report certain instances of cyber fraud (such as where personal data is compromised). ENISA, the European Union Agency for Cybersecurity, have also proposed a wider regime, establishing a centralised database which records cybersecurity incidents as reported (under compulsion) by those companies who have been subject to some form of cyber incident. This would allow a centralised intelligence network of current risks to be built.

The Association of British Insurers has proposed a similar regime. In a report published in November 2019, Economic Crime: Consumer View, the Treasury Committee proposed mandatory reporting of all fraud. Similar regimes are proposed in other jurisdictions. For example, in Australia, the possibility has been mooted of requiring companies to report on ransomware incidents.

The effect of such a regime would be twofold.

First, as has been seen in the USA, the regulations may have the effect of increasing the uptake of cyber insurance policies. Since companies are required to report losses through cyber fraud, they will be eager to show that they took effective pre-emptive steps to protect themselves (or even to avoid publicly reporting an incident by taking steps to prevent their systems being compromised). That said, it is likely that there will be increased uptake of cyber insurance policies in any event, with the example of *AA v Persons Unknown* [2020] 4 WLR 35 demonstrating that insurers will be willing, in the right cases, to commence litigation to recover their subrogated losses.

Second, most directly, there would be greater information available about the current state of cyber fraud, with the possibility of links being drawn between different frauds against different victims. A public – or at least readily accessible – database of payment demands, crypto-asset wallet addresses, emails and modus operandi will greatly assist in both public education and, potentially, collective recovery action by the victims of fraud.

Proceeding against third parties to the fraud

Fourth, new regimes could be accepted by or imposed on third parties to the fraud in order to shift the loss away from the victims.

Alternatively, a development may be led by the banks themselves. The Contingent Reimbursement Model Code for Authorised Push Payment Scams was a strong start in this respect, though was only ever intended as a short term solution – initially until January 2020, though it has evolved since then. Other solutions such as Confirmation of Payee have also been implemented, though again this was not initially the subject of universal adoption and it remains subject to various limitations.

At time of writing, a longer-term solution is still open for debate. It may be that these matters are put on a legislative footing and made compulsory (e.g. as part of the Financial Services and Markets Bill or the Online Safety Bill). In 2021, the Payment Services Regulator identified that the current disparities in voluntary uptake has led to fraudsters either targeting customers of banks who have not opted into voluntary measure or opening accounts with banks which do not respond to COP requests from the remitting bank.

Other options such as a 2.9p transaction fee or industry-wide insurance have been rejected by the banks. The Treasury Committee have recommended that additional protections be built into protections such as COP – such as flagging incorrect spelling, to ensure that customers are not confused by a fraudster using 'soliciter' rather than 'solicitor', for example.

The Regulator has also proposed that banks be subject to an obligation to publish their fraud data, such as their performance in relation to APP scams, reimbursement of victims of fraud, and details of which bank and building society accounts are being used to receive the fraudulent funds. The regulator is exploring whether there should be mandatory intelligence sharing between banks to enhance the detection and prevention of APP scams.

Another proposal, currently under consultation by the PSR, is extending the CRM Code to additional payment service providers such as Indirect PSPs and Indirect Access Providers, or to provide for reimbursement in all but exceptional cases (ie. cases of gross negligence by a non-vulnerable payor or fraud by the payor), or to provide for both remitting and receiving banks to share the cost of reimbursement (subject to a dispute resolution scheme where the banks can contest between themselves the precise allocation). The practical operation of that final dispute resolution scheme could inform the development of the common law on the steps expected of remitting banks under the *Quincecare* duty or the circumstances in which the receiving bank may be liable.

A further possibility, at the moment only at an embryonic stage, is making third parties liable for the costs of the fraud where they are only remotely responsible for it (at least so far as conventional rules on damages are concerned). In their November 2019 Economic Crime report, the Treasury Committee discussed the issue of third parties who hold personal data on individuals being subject to a data breach, with the lost or stolen data then being used by fraudsters to perpetrate frauds on the data subjects. An example was given of an airline which held customer payment information, with the airline being the subject of a data breach and the payment information (at least potentially) being used by the fraudsters. The Treasury Committee proposed that:

> When third parties are responsible for data breaches which lead to associated fraud, they should be responsible for the associated costs. The Government should consider making third parties liable for associated costs to financial services firms and encourage the Information Commission to take this account when fining firms under the General Data Protection Regulations.

This proposal would seem to suggest that the intention is for the victim of the fraud to seek recovery directly from their bank, with the bank then having a right of action against the data controller. However, it is conceivable that (issues of proof aside) the claimant might in due course be granted a direct right of action against the data controller.

A further step from this would be target platforms which fraudsters use to engage with their victims. In real terms, this will be social media platforms, which are frequently used by fraudsters to advertise online investment scams (often also involving crypto-assets). This is not a development which will take place through common law, but it is open to consideration at a legislative level. By contrast with social media platforms, Google changed its rules in August 2021 to force all advertisers of investments to be authorised by the Financial Conduct Authority. This is a change which has been reported as having reduced the incidence of fraud.

Technical developments

Fifth, more immediately, it is likely that new service providers and technological solutions will grow to fulfil the needs of those who are affected by instances of cyber fraud – whether victims, insurers, lawyers, or others. There may be scope for private investigators to provide further assistance in tracing assets and the beneficiaries of shell companies which launder fraudulent proceeds.

Technological solutions may be developed to make use of public data sources to identify likely connections between fraudsters, accessories, banks, and other institutions. For example, products are available which allow a cyber fraud victim to identify the suspected fraudster and be given a list of institutions with which it is believed that the fraudster has an active relationship. This will allow the victim of a cyber fraud to take a more surgical approach to an asset tracing exercise, reducing cost while increasing the likelihood of a positive result.

A particularly good example of deploying technology is in the crypto-asset recovery space, where tools have frequently been deployed in Court to allow litigants to identify where their stolen crypto-assets have been transferred to, including where a manual tracing exercise would be unwieldy or impossible, given the volume and complexity of the data which needs to be input.

Sixth, as technological advances give new tools to the victims of cyber fraud and those who assist them, so too will fraudsters make use of these developments to perpetrate ever more sophisticated frauds.

Currently attracting mainstream attention for spreading misinformation, one such area which may prove relevant is that of 'deepfakes'. 'Deepfakes' are synthetic images or audio, created using a form of machine learning known as deep neural learning. Commonly, deepfakes are video clips which appear to show a person saying or doing something that they never did. Recently, in the first known case of its kind, deepfake audio was presented to a family court to portray one partner as abusive, with the audio appearing to record threats which were simply not made: (2020) 1 IFL 43. The partner's accent, choice of vocabulary and intonation were all convincingly mimicked.

The application of this technology to cyber fraud is obvious. To take just one example, consider the situation where a fraudster sends a false payment instruction, using the email address of the putative payor's CEO. If the recipient decides to telephone the CEO to confirm the instruction, the fraudster could use deepfake technology to mimic the CEO's voice and convincingly confirm the payment instruction. The ramifications of such activity will need to be explored in the future.

Technological advances may provide further opportunities for fraudsters. For example, the Legal Statement on Cryptoassets and Smart Contracts, published on 18 November 2019 by the UK Jurisdiction Taskforce, confirms that electronic signatures should generally be considered valid in English law. Whereas banks could theoretically compare genuine specimen manuscript signatures with a fraudster's forgery, it may be that banks (and other institutions) in the future will need to investigate the circumstances in which a digital signature has been applied to a particular document. Not in the context of fraud, instead concerning the validity of certain guarantees, in Australia a director was found not to have signed a document because the company's practice was for administrative staff to affix the director's signature to particular documents: *Bendigo and Adelaide Bank Limited v Pickard* [2019] SASC 123.

Seventh, rather than technological advances providing cyber fraudsters with more tools or victims with more defences, it may be that new technologies and ways of doing business may create new opportunities for cyber fraud.

One example may be interference with smart contracts, where certain actions automatically execute on the occurrence of events which are pre-defined in the coding of the smart contract. The Singapore case of *B2C2 v Quoine* [2019] SGHC(I) 03 (on appeal, [2020] SGCA(I) 02) did not concern fraud. Rather, two parties were transacting with one another exclusively through the medium of a smart contract with no human intervention. During the course of the contract, a circumstance – unforeseen at time of contracting – arose that resulted in the parties automatically executing transactions which were at dramatically above market value. However, as such transactions become more frequent, it is almost inevitable that a cyber fraudster will seek to interfere with them. For example, in circumstance such as in *B2C2*, what if the fraudster, rather than an accidental oversight, caused the relevant program to be unable to access the relevant market data (which was the root cause of the trades in *B2C2*)?

Other examples are restricted only by the technology currently available. New developments provide new opportunities for fraud. For example, the Post Office will now issue stamps with a barcode, which will direct a reader to a customisable message set by the sender of the letter. However, this gives rise to the possibility of fraudsters interfering with that customisable message, relying on the authenticity of the letter to persuade the receipient to believe that the digital message also originated with the sender.

Broader impact of cyber fraud

Eighth, looking at litigation as a whole, the impact that cyber fraud has on court or arbitration processes more generally will need to be explored. Consider the morally bankrupt litigant who is prepared to obtain illicit access to the computer system of a judge or arbitrator and therefore see a draft of the judgment or award being produced by that person. That litigant may then be able to adjust their actions accordingly. For example, if it is apparent that the judgment or award is against them, the litigant may dissipate their assets (perhaps notwithstanding a freezing injunction) or make a tactical settlement offer to the other side. Even when an embargoed judgment is circulated to the parties, a cyber fraudster might obtain access to that document and thereby take action – for example, by taking a position in respect of the publicly-listed shares of one of the parties in anticipation of the judgment affecting the share price.

These particular examples are not yet known to have happened, but there are similar examples which have happened. In 2022, an arbitrator found that an arbitrating party had obtained illicit access to the arbitration counterparty's email account, using that illicit access to generate a fraudulent email which the first party then relied on as evidence in the arbitration: *London Arbitration 28/22* (2022) 1114 LMLN. In 2015, the Permanent Court of Arbitration's website pages for a marine border dispute was compromised by a cyber-attack, which had the potential to allow the wrongdoers to access the networks of law firms and media organisations. In 2008, a party to an arbitration intercepted materials which were privileged to its counterparty: *Libananco Holdings v Republic of Turkey* ICSID Case No. ARB/06/8.

Other examples of issues where interception of confidential or privileged lines of communication by other litigants or third parties include accessing telephone or video hearings, or intercepting live messaging services which allow representatives of a party to conduct discussions or mark-up documents (being common, for example, in arbitrations where live transcripts are available).

In any event, the need for effective cyber security is something which those in the industry are aware of. Some initial steps have been taken to address this perceived risk. In late 2019, a working group set up by the International Council for Commercial Arbitration published the Cybersecurity Protocol for International Arbitration (2020) to give appropriate cybersecurity guidance to users of arbitration, counsel, arbitrators and arbitral institutions.

Ninth, there is scope for a specialist division or list to deal with cyber fraud (or wider cyber) matters. In the first edition of this guide, reference was made to a government announcement in 2018 that a specialist fraud, cybercrime and economic crime court would open in London in 2025. There has been little public news on the proposed new court, but the idea of concentrating expertise in such matters (including in the detailed operation of complex new technologies, such as crypto-assets stored on a blockchain) has obvious attractions. At present, cyber fraud litigation is taking place in various divisions of the High Court. Although there is naturally cross-fertilisation of ideas between the divisions, a clearer direction as to which list cyber fraud maters should be directed to – or even a specialist list – would be worth exploring.

MORE BOOKS BY LAW BRIEF PUBLISHING

A selection of our other titles available now:-

'A Practical Guide to Parental Alienation in Private and Public Law Children Cases' by Sam King QC & Frankie Shama
'Contested Heritage – Removing Art from Land and Historic Buildings' by Richard Harwood QC, Catherine Dobson, David Sawtell
'The Limits of Separate Legal Personality: When Those Running a Company Can Be Held Personally Liable for Losses Caused to Third Parties Outside of the Company' by Dr Mike Wilkinson
'A Practical Guide to Transgender Law' by Robin Moira White & Nicola Newbegin
'Artificial Intelligence – The Practical Legal Issues (2nd Edition)' by John Buyers
'A Practical Guide to Residential Freehold Conveyancing' by Lorraine Richardson
'A Practical Guide to Pensions on Divorce for Lawyers' by Bryan Scant
'A Practical Guide to Challenging Sham Marriage Allegations in Immigration Law' by Priya Solanki
'A Practical Guide to Legal Rights in Scotland' by Sarah-Jane Macdonald
'A Practical Guide to New Build Conveyancing' by Paul Sams & Rebecca East
'A Practical Guide to Defending Barristers in Disciplinary Cases' by Marc Beaumont
'A Practical Guide to Inherited Wealth on Divorce' by Hayley Trim
'A Practical Guide to Practice Direction 12J and Domestic Abuse in Private Law Children Proceedings' by Rebecca Cross & Malvika Jaganmohan
'A Practical Guide to Confiscation and Restraint' by Narita Bahra QC, John Carl Townsend, David Winch
'A Practical Guide to the Law of Forests in Scotland' by Philip Buchan
'A Practical Guide to Health and Medical Cases in Immigration Law' by Rebecca Chapman & Miranda Butler
'A Practical Guide to Bad Character Evidence for Criminal Practitioners by Aparna Rao
'A Practical Guide to Extradition Law post-Brexit' by Myles Grandison et al

'A Practical Guide to Hoarding and Mental Health for Housing Lawyers' by Rachel Coyle
'A Practical Guide to Psychiatric Claims in Personal Injury – 2nd Edition' by Liam Ryan
'Stephens on Contractual Indemnities' by Richard Stephens
'A Practical Guide to the EU Succession Regulation' by Richard Frimston
'A Practical Guide to Solicitor and Client Costs – 2nd Edition' by Robin Dunne
'Constructive Dismissal – Practice Pointers and Principles' by Benjimin Burgher
'A Practical Guide to Religion and Belief Discrimination Claims in the Workplace' by Kashif Ali
'A Practical Guide to the Law of Medical Treatment Decisions' by Ben Troke
'Fundamental Dishonesty and QOCS in Personal Injury Proceedings: Law and Practice' by Jake Rowley
'A Practical Guide to the Law in Relation to School Exclusions' by Charlotte Hadfield & Alice de Coverley
'A Practical Guide to Divorce for the Silver Separators' by Karin Walker
'The Right to be Forgotten – The Law and Practical Issues' by Melissa Stock
'A Practical Guide to Planning Law and Rights of Way in National Parks, the Broads and AONBs' by James Maurici QC, James Neill et al
'A Practical Guide to Election Law' by Tom Tabori
'A Practical Guide to the Law in Relation to Surrogacy' by Andrew Powell
'A Practical Guide to Claims Arising from Fatal Accidents – 2nd Edition' by James Patience
'A Practical Guide to the Ownership of Employee Inventions – From Entitlement to Compensation' by James Tumbridge & Ashley Roughton
'A Practical Guide to Asbestos Claims' by Jonathan Owen & Gareth McAloon
'A Practical Guide to Stamp Duty Land Tax in England and Northern Ireland' by Suzanne O'Hara
'A Practical Guide to the Law of Farming Partnerships' by Philip Whitcomb
'Covid-19, Homeworking and the Law – The Essential Guide to Employment and GDPR Issues' by Forbes Solicitors
'Covid-19 and Criminal Law – The Essential Guide' by Ramya Nagesh
'Covid-19 and Family Law in England and Wales – The Essential Guide' by Safda Mahmood

'A Practical Guide to the Law of Unlawful Eviction and Harassment – 2nd Edition' by Stephanie Lovegrove
'Covid-19, Brexit and the Law of Commercial Leases – The Essential Guide' by Mark Shelton
'A Practical Guide to Costs in Personal Injury Claims – 2nd Edition' by Matthew Hoe
'A Practical Guide to the General Data Protection Regulation (GDPR) – 2nd Edition' by Keith Markham
'Ellis on Credit Hire – Sixth Edition' by Aidan Ellis & Tim Kevan
'A Practical Guide to Working with Litigants in Person and McKenzie Friends in Family Cases' by Stuart Barlow
'Protecting Unregistered Brands: A Practical Guide to the Law of Passing Off' by Lorna Brazell
'A Practical Guide to Secondary Liability and Joint Enterprise Post-Jogee' by Joanne Cecil & James Mehigan
'A Practical Guide to the Pre-Action RTA Claims Protocol for Personal Injury Lawyers' by Antonia Ford
'A Practical Guide to Neighbour Disputes and the Law' by Alexander Walsh
'A Practical Guide to Forfeiture of Leases' by Mark Shelton
'A Practical Guide to Coercive Control for Legal Practitioners and Victims' by Rachel Horman
'A Practical Guide to Rights Over Airspace and Subsoil' by Daniel Gatty
'Tackling Disclosure in the Criminal Courts – A Practitioner's Guide' by Narita Bahra QC & Don Ramble
'A Practical Guide to the Law of Driverless Cars – Second Edition' by Alex Glassbrook, Emma Northey & Scarlett Milligan
'A Practical Guide to TOLATA Claims' by Greg Williams
'A Practical Guide to Elderly Law – 2nd Edition' by Justin Patten
'A Practical Guide to Responding to Housing Disrepair and Unfitness Claims' by Iain Wightwick
'A Practical Guide to the Construction and Rectification of Wills and Trust Instruments' by Edward Hewitt
'A Practical Guide to the Law of Bullying and Harassment in the Workplace' by Philip Hyland
'How to Be a Freelance Solicitor: A Practical Guide to the SRA-Regulated Freelance Solicitor Model' by Paul Bennett

'A Practical Guide to Prison Injury Claims' by Malcolm Johnson
'A Practical Guide to the Small Claims Track - 2nd Edition' by Dominic Bright
'A Practical Guide to Advising Clients at the Police Station' by Colin Stephen McKeown-Beaumont
'A Practical Guide to Antisocial Behaviour Injunctions' by Iain Wightwick
'Practical Mediation: A Guide for Mediators, Advocates, Advisers, Lawyers, and Students in Civil, Commercial, Business, Property, Workplace, and Employment Cases' by Jonathan Dingle with John Sephton
'The Mini-Pupillage Workbook' by David Boyle
'A Practical Guide to Crofting Law' by Brian Inkster
'A Practical Guide to Spousal Maintenance' by Liz Cowell
'A Practical Guide to the Law of Domain Names and Cybersquatting' by Andrew Clemson
'A Practical Guide to the Law of Gender Pay Gap Reporting' by Harini Iyengar
'A Practical Guide to the Rights of Grandparents in Children Proceedings' by Stuart Barlow
'NHS Whistleblowing and the Law' by Joseph England
'Employment Law and the Gig Economy' by Nigel Mackay & Annie Powell
'A Practical Guide to Noise Induced Hearing Loss (NIHL) Claims' by Andrew Mckie, Ian Skeate, Gareth McAloon
'An Introduction to Beauty Negligence Claims – A Practical Guide for the Personal Injury Practitioner' by Greg Almond
'Intercompany Agreements for Transfer Pricing Compliance' by Paul Sutton
'Zen and the Art of Mediation' by Martin Plowman
'A Practical Guide to the SRA Principles, Individual and Law Firm Codes of Conduct 2019 – What Every Law Firm Needs to Know' by Paul Bennett
'A Practical Guide to Adoption for Family Lawyers' by Graham Pegg
'A Practical Guide to Industrial Disease Claims' by Andrew Mckie & Ian Skeate
'A Practical Guide to Redundancy' by Philip Hyland
'A Practical Guide to Vicarious Liability' by Mariel Irvine
'A Practical Guide to Applications for Landlord's Consent and Variation of Leases' by Mark Shelton
'A Practical Guide to Relief from Sanctions Post-Mitchell and Denton' by Peter Causton

www.ingramcontent.com/pod-product-compliance
Ingram Content Group UK Ltd.
Pitfield, Milton Keynes, MK11 3LW, UK
UKHW020142290926
15471UKWH00004B/648

9 781914 608889